Why Do the Swiss Have Such Great Sex?

Extraordinary Answers to 66 Improbable Questions About Switzerland

Why Do the Swiss Have Such Great Sex?

*Extraordinary Answers to 66 Improbable
Questions About Switzerland*

ASHLEY CURTIS

Bergli

First edition
© 2018 Bergli Books, all rights reserved
© Text Ashley Curtis
European Edition, ISBN 978-3-03869-047-4 :
Printed in the Czech Republic
International edition, ISBN 978-3-03869-058-0
Also available as an ebook. Epub ISBN 978-3-03869-059-7.
Mobi ISBN 978-3-03869-060-3.
Also available in German: *Warum Haben die Schweizer so grossartigen Sex?* ISBN 0978-3-03869-048-1

Bergli Books received a grant from the Swiss Federal Office of Culture 2016–2018
For a list of sources, see www.bergli.ch/Why?Sources.
www.bergli.ch

Table of Contents

1

Why Do the Swiss Have Such Great Sex?

In 2013 the market research and data analytics firm YouGov carried out a widely reported survey of sex lives in 13 European countries. YouGov is a highly respected sampler of opinions, and its CEO has an illustrious name: Shakespeare. The *Guardian* newspaper has dubbed Shakespeare "the pollster with the uncanny ability of getting it right."[1]

And who came out on top? Latin lovers? Liberated Dutch? The tabloid-loving Brits? None of it. Switzerland had the highest ratings both of "my sexual performance" and "the quality of my sex life," ahead of Spain, Italy, the Scandinavian countries, and, in last place, Shakespeare's homeland. The Swiss tabloid *Blick* (June 24th, 2013) celebrated this astonishing victory with a splashy headline: "We are the Sex Masters!"

Two years later an article in the online journal *Alternet*, which was based on a whole slew of different surveys, listed

---

1   In 2001, YouGov predicted Labour's general election victory to within one percentage point. In 2017, it correctly predicted a hung parliament for the general election—a description that the *Guardian* described as "certainly brave," and which was also certainly correct.

the top twelve most sexually satisfied countries "in no particular order," but with the Swiss as the first nation on the list. This led to an explosion of reports (*The Independent, The Mirror, Salon, Metro News, Elite Readers,* etc.) claiming that the Swiss were the number one lovers in the world. "Switzerland is both hot and safe," reported the online women's magazine *Bustle.* The news made it all the way to India, where the Internet media and news company *Scoopwhoop* asked, "Is it the picturesque landscape? Is it the romantic Yash Raj movies? Is it the sex education programs they start from kindergarten itself?"[2]

These excellent results from 2013 and 2015 were all the more remarkable for the vast improvement Swiss lovers had obviously made since April 18th, 2012, when the same *Blick* displayed the devastating headline: "What a Defeat: Swiss are Losers in Bed!" This time it was reporting on a *C-Date* survey that revealed Brazilian men and Italian women as the world's best lovers, and put the Swiss unceremoniously in *last place.*

If Switzerland can move from last place to first in a single year, you might wonder what ups and downs it has experienced throughout the centuries. So let's have a peek.

Six hundred years ago, in 1417, the papal secretary Poggio Bracciolini—a man who fathered 14 children with his mistress and another 6 with his wife—visited the baths at Baden in Canton Aargau and filed this report:

---

2   How the 75 Hindi films produced by the Indian entertainment company Yash Raj might have contributed to Swiss sexual prowess remains somewhat obscure, but Switzerland's unlikely reputation as a land of lovers has clearly penetrated all the way to India.

These baths are the general resort of lovers and their mistresses, of all, in short, who are fond of pleasure. Many ladies pretend to be sick, merely with a view of being sent for cure to this watering place. You consequently see here a great number of handsome females without their husbands and not protected by any male relations, but attended by a couple of maids and a man-servant, or some elderly cousin, who is very easily given the slip . . . I believe there are no baths in the world more efficacious in promoting the propagation of the human species . . . I think this must be the place where the first man was created, which the Hebrews call the garden of pleasure.

This must have been one of those good years—even better, perhaps, than 2013. Poggio made some more remarkable observations:

Here we meet with abbots, monks, friars, and priests, who live with greater license than the rest of the company. These ecclesiastics, forgetting the gravity of their profession, sometimes bathe with the ladies, and adorn their hair with silken ribbons.

Two centuries after Poggio's visit, the Swiss were still living it up in Baden. Thomas Coryat, a British traveler and court jester at the time of a more famous Shakespeare than the pollster, was shocked and befuddled by the baths—suggesting, perhaps, that 1608 was another of those bad years for the Brits.

But let these Germans and Helvetians do as they list, and observe these kind of wanton customs as long as they will; for mine own part were I a married man, and meant to spend some little time here with my wife for solace and recreation sake, truly I should hardly be persuaded to suffer her to bathe herself naked in one and the self-same bath with one only bachelor or married man with her, because if she was fair, and had an attractive countenance, she might perhaps cornify [cuckold] me.

Yet Swiss sex also had its less exciting periods. In 1685 the future Bishop of Salisbury, Gilbert Burnet, was in Bern and noted that, "The third adultery is punished with death, which is also the punishment for the fifth act of fornication."[3] Burnet observed the execution of a woman who "confessed herself guilty of many whoredoms," and he found it a very tender beheading:

The Advoyer, after the sentence [was read], took the criminal very gently by the hand, and prayed for her soul; and after execution there was a sermon for the instruction of the people.

According to Burnet, however, adultery and fornication were not common. An "eminent physician" had told him that the Bernese women, even those of high rank, did all their housework themselves, and so

among them the blood was cleansed by their labour; and as that made them sleep well, so they did not amuse themselves with much thinking, nor did they know what Amours were.

---

3   Today close to 40 percent of Swiss adults have had sex with more than ten people. If post-Reformation Bernese justice were still being consequently administered, there wouldn't be many Swiss left alive.

Up in the Alps, meanwhile, fornication was also frowned upon—but only when the sun was up. After dark it might be time for a *Kiltgang*. *Kiltgang* literally means evening walk, but my dictionary gives it a more colorful definition: "a traditional nightly tryst of love in rural Switzerland." The Swiss painter Franz Niklaus König provides a picture from 1814:

The Kiltgang *is a deeply rooted and intractable custom in Canton Bern. The young men secretly visit the girls at night—sometimes alone, sometimes in groups. The way in is via the window; first, however, protestations of tenderness are delivered, often in a comical enough style; these are followed by a kind of capitulation. When the young man has finally made it [up the ladder and] into the girl's room, he is refreshed with some kirsch. From here on it all proceeds, so they say, with the utmost politeness and respectability! I'd love to believe this, but it just won't lodge in my brain: a rustic mountaineer going through all this rigmarole for some platonic entertainment? For this he has climbed a rough mountain path, for three or four hours, through rain and wind, as is often the case? Besides, there are afterwards frequently symptoms of these visits, and they hardly seem platonic, though happily they generally lead in the direction of the church.*

The church battled for centuries against the *Kiltgang*, but to no avail. Villagers tacitly accepted the practice—partly because a premarital pregnancy was just the thing to confirm a couple's ability to do what was existential for mountain peasants: have children.

In 1836 a well-known hatter in Canton Glarus published *Eros: the Male Love of the Greeks*—the first monograph on gay sex in the modern western world. Heinrich Hössli was way ahead of his time in arguing that homosexuality should not be punished as a crime, treated as an illness, or damned as a sin.[4] *Who's Who in Gay and Lesbian History* seconds Hössli's biographer in judging his book "the most important work on male love since Plato's *Symposium*." A good year for Swiss sex? Yes and no. *Eros* was banned by cantonal authorities, and most extant copies were incinerated in the Glarus conflagration (see Question 13). Hössli himself, once sought out as a milliner with an incisive eye for female fashion, died an embittered and impoverished vagrant.

In Switzerland as elsewhere in Europe, the end of the 19th century saw a growing awareness of abuses in the widespread practice of prostitution. Impoverished women, teenagers, and even child sex slaves were brutally exploited by pimps and their customers. On the other side, government authorities resorted to forced gynecological examinations (known as "steel rape") of lower-class women suspected of being prostitutes—in order to find and lock up those who were diseased, and thereby safeguard the venereal health of the male (and especially the military) population. In reaction to these abuses a Social Purity Movement, largely driven by women, sprang up in Switzerland, but at first fought only for the forcible repression of prostitution and the deportation of foreign sex workers. Around the turn of the century the movement became gentler, and the focus shifted from criminalization to education and social assistance. This "education," however, fo-

---

4   In 1942, just over 100 years after the appearance of Hössli's book, Switzerland did decriminalize homosexuality—beating out England (1967), Germany (1969), Finland (1971) and Spain (1979), but losing out to Vatican City (!) and Italy (both 1890), and getting creamed by France (1791). Cantons Ticino, Valais and Vaud, however, were way ahead of the game—they made the move in 1798.

cused on abstinence, the banning of dances and parties, and the censorship of literature and films. As after the Reformation, sex itself became the bad guy, and "great sex" an oxymoron.

A century later, and another flip—or flop. Prostitution has been legal in Switzerland since 1942, and sex work is a 3.5 billion franc industry. Earnings are taxed, and the workers contribute to and benefit from social insurance. In Zurich, government-constructed Sex Boxes provide infrastructure for the trade: a drive-in facility, where you can have sex in your car with a waiting prostitute, also features a café, a laundry, and showers for the workers.

As for education, today it's of another order than that imagined by the purity campaigners. In Basel, in 2011, Sex Boxes of a different kind from those in Zurich found their way into kindergarten. Tactile tools for sex-ed, they contained, among other items, a wooden penis and a plush vagina. Parents concerned about social purity initiated legal proceedings against the schools, but were brusquely rebuffed by the Supreme Court, which wrote that

> it is obvious, that being informed about the basic terms and connections of the human body and sexuality fundamentally supports the publicly acknowledged goal of preventing sexual molestation and of protecting health.

Swiss sexual education seems to work: Switzerland has the lowest teen pregnancy rate in the world—one-seventh that of the US, one-sixth that of Britain, a third the rate in France, and half that of the Netherlands.

In another sign of the times the "Last Sex Shop Before the Jungfrau," which opened its doors 20 years ago on the main street in Interlaken, reports that its clientele has evolved in the direction of equality. While at the start customers were 80 percent male, the sexes are now evenly represented: emancipation, perhaps, in another sense than that intended by the feminist abstinence campaigners a hundred years ago.

It is not surprising that sexual mores should vary over the centuries, but we are still left with that inexplicable jump in Swiss loving from 2012 to 2013. For an explanation we can turn to Swiss sex expert Caroline Fux[5]. Fux, a psychologist who answers distraught questions about sex and relationships in a column in *Blick* read by half a million Swiss every day, has a simple explanation:

> *There are certainly surveys about how different countries perform in bed, but most of them are not at all scientific. A lot of what are sold as serious studies are completely unfounded nonsense.*

Completely unfounded nonsense might explain a lot here. Especially those dismal results arrived at by *C-Date*, which, now that I look it up, I find is far from a serious research institution—rather, it's an online tool for hooking up. (The "C" stands for casual.) But is Ms. Fux really ready to throw away the data collected by Shakespeare, the man with the "uncanny ability of getting it right?" Not necessarily. Here is Fux's take on Swiss lovemaking:

> *The image of the Swiss is not exactly that of superlative lovers. We actually tend to stand as opposites to the classic*

---

5   Yes, this is her real name.—though in German Fux rhymes with books rather than bucks.

Latin types. However, I would say that Swiss lovers are prag-matic, and in a positive way. They have a good sexual educa-tion, a lot of knowledge—and this is not to be underrated when considering sexual competence. In addition, we Swiss are very open about sex. We are emancipated, and therefore care a lot that the sex is good for both partners. Thus you shouldn't underestimate Swiss lovers—they're the outsiders who you suddenly find have qualified for the finals.

No Latin lovers, but the outsiders who qualify for the finals. If you're looking for a raffish opera star to sweep you away on a motorcycle, you might want to head south. Great sex is after all a matter of taste—but also, unfortunately, often a matter of delusion. What really makes sex great, according to yet an-other survey—this time by Durex and YourTango—might not be riding on that motorcycle. Here's a Durex spokesman reviewing their 2013 poll:

When people think of great sex, many often conjure up im-ages of one-night-stands or Spring Break. Our research shows the contrary, that when you are with someone who wants only you, you feel confident enough to try out new things and express your fantasies, which in turn leads to more intimacy and even better sex between partners.

YourTango CEO Andrea Miller agrees.

We've been conditioned by the media to believe that sex is primarily physical and a couple's sex life will inevitably fizzle with time. However, these findings indicate just the opposite—getting closer on an emotional level is the key to getting closer physically.

If Durex and YourTango are right, then it's good love that makes good loving—which has nothing to do with Brazilian lovers, Italian lovers, Swiss lovers, or lovers from Mars. And, wonder of wonders, it's what we might have expected from the beginning. Nations don't have sex, after all—people do.

2

Could a Tsunami Strike Switzerland?

The Tauredenum Event could be the title of a disaster movie. And a disaster it was, but not a movie—yet. Here is a description from the contemporary chronicler Gregory of Tours in his *History of the Franks*. The year is 563.

> *A great prodigy appeared in Gaul at the fortress of Taure-denum, which was situated on high ground above the River Rhône. Here a curious bellowing sound was heard for more than sixty days: then the whole hillside was split open and separated from the mountain nearest to it, and it fell into the river, carrying with it men, churches, property and houses. The banks of the river were blocked and the water flowed backwards. The water flooded the higher reaches and submerged and carried everything which was on its banks.*
>
> *And yet again the inhabitants were taken unawares: as the accumulated water suddenly broke through the blockage, it drowned those who lived lower down, just as it had done higher up, destroying their houses, killing their cattle, and carrying away and overwhelming with its violent and*

unexpected inundation everything which stood on its banks as far as the city of Geneva. It is told by many that the mass of water was so great that it went over the walls of the city.

In 2012 geophysicists at the University of Geneva published a paper analyzing huge deposits of sediment near where the Rhône enters the lake. Their conclusion was that the Tauredenum event involved a massive landslide that caused a collapse of the Rhône delta and a slippage of sediment at the eastern end of the lake, and this in turn created a tsunami. A 13-meter high wave, traveling at 70 kilometers per hour, would have reached Lausanne 15 minutes after the slippage. Three quarters of an hour after that, its height reduced to 8 meters, it would have inundated Geneva, crashing over the city walls just as Gregory reported.

The Swiss Seismological Service agrees. It catalogues several tsunamis that have crossed Swiss lakes and inflicted widespread devastation. An earthquake near Aigle set off a tsunami in Lake Geneva in 1584. In 1601 an earthquake caused submarine landslides in Lake Luzern, and a 4 meter high wave engulfed the city. Luzern was hit again in 1681, this time with a 5-meter tsunami. And in 1806 the Goldau landslide, which destroyed the village of that name and killed 500 of its inhabitants, unleashed a 10-meter high wall of water in Lake Laurerz.

Today there are over a million people living on low-lying land around Lake Geneva. And it turns out that the Tauredenum event was not a one-off. In fact,

The sedimentary record of the deep basin of Lake Geneva, in combination with the historical record, show that during the past 3,695 years, at least six tsunamis were generated

by mass movements, indicating that the tsunami hazard in the Lake Geneva region should not be neglected . . . We believe that the risk associated with tsunamis in lakes is currently underestimated, and that these phenomena require greater attention if future catastrophes are to be avoided.

So wrote the Geneva geophysicists, who calculated that we can expect a tsunami on Lake Geneva, on average, once every 625 years.

A big one happened in 563. A small one in 1584. Now it's 2018. Do the math.

Next time you're in Geneva, don't just worry about what's going on in the Large Hadron Collider out by the airport (see Question 9). Keep an eye on that big lake as well—for an only partly unexpected "event."

3

How Many Lives Does a Tunnel Cost?

On June 8th, 2000, a 40 kg metal rod fell down a shaft and struck dead a 33-year old German worker.

On December 21st, 2005, the last two cars of a trolley carrying rubble jumped the track and set a service car rolling. The service car crushed two Italian workers, 24 and 31 years old. One of them was due to be a father in three months' time; the other was finishing his last planned day of work.

On March 13th, 2001, a 23-year-old South African worker was buried under a pile of rubble.

On April 3rd, 2003, a German worker was struck dead by a falling block of stone.

In autumn of 2003, a 37-year-old Austrian worker, father of a small boy, was run over by a rolling spool of heavy cable.

On November 23rd, 2006, a German worker was crushed by a trolley wagon. He left a wife and small child.

On June 24th, 2010, a 46-year-old German engineer died after falling from a transport train.

On June 16th, 2012, a Sicilian worker fell to his death from a piece of scaffolding.

* * *

The deaths described above occurred during work on the Gotthard Base tunnel—at 57.1 kilometers, the longest traffic tunnel in the world. It cost one life for every 6.3 kilometers. For comparison, the Eurotunnel under the English Channel cost one life for every 4.6 kilometers. The Lötschberg Base Tunnel between Cantons Bern and Valais has cost one life for every 6.9 kilometers so far, but it hasn't been completely finished, so that toll may rise.

Traveling back in time, things get distinctly worse. The Simplon tunnel between Brig and Iselle, which was the world's longest for 77 years, cost 67 lives, or about one for every 300 meters of track. Its predecessor as the world record holder, the *first* Gotthard train tunnel, cost 199 lives (See Question 22). This tunnel, still used as an alternative to the new Base Tunnel, takes about 8 minutes to ride through on a train. Every *two seconds* of the ride corresponds to the death of a worker.

One dead worker for every two seconds, however, is a vast underestimate, because it only includes deaths which occurred during actual work on the site. Many, many others died due to pathologies directly attributable to their work on the tunnel, or to the workers' atrociously unsanitary living conditions— pathologies such as hookworm, typhus and silicosis (also known, pleasantly, as *grinder's asthma, miner's phthisis* or *potter's rot*).

Hookworm rarely kills on its own, but it severely weakens you through abdominal pain, diarrhea, weight loss, and anemia, making you more vulnerable to other diseases. Typhus leads to fever, a full body rash, inflammation of the brain, altered mental states, coma and death. Both of these commonly arise when living conditions are unsanitary. Silicosis, on the other hand, is earned in the tunnel through inhalation of crystalline silica dust. It can result in the rapid onset of a chronic and debilitating cough and shortness of breath, weakness and weight loss, lung scarring, fever, a gradual darkening of the skin until the upper body is bluish, rifts and cracks in fingernails and toenails, heart disease and death. Silicosis can develop up to 10 years after exposure to the dust.

The deaths due to work on the transit tunnels mentioned above will be seen by many as "justified" by the convenience the tunnels provide both for travel and trade. Harder to justify are deaths on train lines that are useful for neither. The cog railway up to the Jungfraujoch, derided by the British minister to Switzerland in 1905 as an "insensate" and "vulgarizing" scheme, and by a Swiss senator as a "speculating, greedy, all-consuming golden Moloch," cost 30 Italian lives for just over 7 kilometers of tunnel. Buying a full-price round-trip ticket from the Kleine Scheidegg today, you'll be paying this golden Moloch 4.27 Swiss francs per dead Italian worker.

An "Indian Buffet" at the Bollywood Restaurant at the Jungfraujoch, on the other hand, will set you back SFr 32.50.

Life is cheap at the "Top of Europe."

4

Could Swiss Gold Sink the Swiss Navy?

"He's the admiral of the Swiss Navy" is a way of putting down a pompous, self-important fellow. Yet the Swiss navy does exist—sort of. It's even being refurbished. Fourteen new patrol boats—made in Finland—will be arriving between 2019 and 2021, each equipped with a fully automatic 12.7 millimeter cannon for taking out lightly armored vehicles on land and water, as well as low-flying helicopters. The navy—technically, *Motorboat Company 10*—defends Swiss borders against enemies who might attack from Germany, France and Italy on, respectively, Lake Constance, Lake Geneva, and Lakes Lugano and Maggiore. Strangely enough, however, the navy trains on Lake Luzern—directly in the middle of land-locked Switzerland. From here the boats can be transported on trucks to the lakes they might actually need to defend.

Each of the fourteen *Patrol Boat 16*s weighs 9 tons, and has a maximum carrying capacity of 1 ton more. The Swiss National Bank, meanwhile, owns 1,040 tons of gold bullion, worth 41 billion francs, in bars half the size of a loaf of bread weighing 12 kilograms each. Most of the bullion is stored in a top-secret location—which happens to be, as a reporter from the *Bund* newspaper discovered in 2008, directly under the Government Plaza in Bern. The Government Plaza is itself directly in front of the Federal Palace, where the Parliament and Federal Council meet. In summer the plaza becomes a water-park, with 26 fountains shooting variable jets of water directly out of the gneiss pavement. Half-naked children play in the water, while underneath them precious gold sits in a vault the size of half the plaza and extending down, down, down—dozens of meters straight down—almost to the level of the Aare River.

The gold of Bern was stolen once—in one of the greatest thefts in history. In 1798 Napoleon's troops, having conquered the city, made their way into the treasury and confiscated its treasure for their leader—to the tune of 126 million of today's Euros. The French transported the gold in several columns of wagons to Paris, where it was melted down, turned to French francs, and used to pay the army.

If a Napoleon of today were to loot the Bernese treasury, he would enter the vault below the sopping children and find 728 tons of bullion. (Perhaps because they learned a lesson in 1798, the Swiss today keep 30 percent of their reserves in the Banks of Canada and England.) With the Aare so near, our new Napoleon might be tempted to transport it via water. Having conquered Switzerland, he would have the Swiss Navy in his pocket—so why not use the *Patrol Boat 16*s of *Motorboat Company 10*?

Well, here's why. You're talking 52 tons of gold per boat. Since gold is extremely dense—each liter weighs over 19 kilograms—you could fit it onto the boats without too much of a problem: each boat would get a neat cube of the shiny stuff,

140 centimeters on a side. These little 52-ton cubes, however, would immediately sink the entire Swiss Navy. Napoleon IV's gold would end up on the bottom of the Aare, and would be of little use for paying his troops.

You might think that gold in water like this would be a novelty—after all, who would store gold in a river? But not all Swiss gold is owned by the National Bank. A 2017 study by the Federal Institute of Aquatic Science and Technology found that there are 1.5 million francs worth of gold in a most surprising and very wet location: Swiss sewage. This gold is concentrated in the sludge of the Jura (where the Swiss watch industry is based) and the Ticino (where two-thirds of the world's raw gold is refined). It doesn't smell very nice, but hey—1.5 million francs is nothing to sneeze at.

Which gives me an idea. Since the location of the Government Plaza gold has been leaked, and we don't really want to sink the Swiss Navy, the Swiss National Bank might think of hiding it in a very smelly, highly unattractive place. I won't spell it out in case criminals are reading this, but I've probably said enough to make my idea clear to the astute reader.

And just one more thing about gold and water: if you were to hammer out all of the Swiss National Bank's gold bullion until it was very thin—one ten thousandth of a millimeter—you could do a remarkable thing with it. And before you say that it's impossible to make such a thin gold foil, let me inform you that it's not impossible at all—and that, in fact, it was gold foil of just this thickness that allowed the Nobel Prize-winning physicist Ernest Rutherford, back in 1911, to discover the structure of the atom.

Once we've hammered it out, we could take our very thin layer of Swiss gold and lay it on top of some water—to be precise, on top of Lake Geneva. It would almost exactly fit. It might wreak havoc in the financial markets, and you'd want to gather it in before the next tsunami—but on a nice evening, you'd really have a golden sunset on the lake.

5

What Happens To a Corpse in a Crevasse?

You've died on, or in, a glacier. You're alone—or perhaps there are no survivors of your party left to call the REGA (Swiss Air Rescue) to haul you out. Perhaps you've fallen into a deep crevasse, but maybe you've been buried in a storm or an avalanche, or have died of exposure or trauma on the surface of the ice.

If you don't get eaten as carrion by a fox, an eagle or a vulture, one of two things can happen to your corpse. The first of these occurs to those bodies, or parts of bodies, that are in a moist environment sealed off from oxygen—in our case, inside the ice of the glacier, or in the frigid water at the bottom of a crevasse. This process is called saponification, which literally means "turning into soap." The organs and soft tissues of your body will change into a wax-like, fatty substance called "adipocere" or "corpse wax"—sometimes gray and sometimes tan, depending on the color of your blubber.

You can make good candles out of adipocere. When the English physician Augustus Granville gave a public lecture on dissecting a mummy in 1825, he lit his talk with candles he had made himself—from what he presumed was wax used to preserve the mummy. In fact, his lecture was lit by the mummy's own saponified fat.

Granville's mistake shows us that mummification—our second process—and saponification can both happen to the same corpse. In contrast to saponification, mummification occurs when a body dries out. This happens when it's on the surface of a glacier, subject to dry air and glacial winds. The soft tissues shrink and the skin becomes hard and leathery. If you're half-buried in dense snow your body can do both tricks at once: mummify above the snow and saponify below it.

A mummified body can survive for thousands of years—as long as it's kept cold. Such was the fate of the "Ice-Man," Ötzi, who was frozen for over 5 millennia in the upper reaches of the Niederjochferner glacier on the Austrian-Italian border. When Ötzi emerged from the ice in 1991, a woman from Zurich falsely identified his 5,000-year-old corpse as that of her father, who had been missing for only a decade. That's how well Ötzi was preserved.

Ötzi's situation was unusual for a glacial corpse—he had been buried at a flat spot at the very top of the glacier, a place where the ice didn't flow down the mountain. By 1991 all the ice above him had simply melted away. Your corpse would most likely not be so immobile, for most glacier ice does move, and in complicated ways.

Glaciers don't only flow down mountains like very slow molasses—the ice within them also moves in a vertical direction relative to the surface. Since snow is always accumulating, and then turning to ice, at the upper reaches of a glacier, anything sitting there—like your corpse—will get progressively more deeply buried. Thus while you're being carried toward the valley by the glacier's flow, you're at the same time sinking deeper and deeper into the glacier's gut.

The lower end of the glacier, where more ice is melting than accumulating, is known as the ablation zone. Anything inside the glacier here rises slowly to the surface, and anything already on the surface stays there. So if you die in the accumulation zone, whether you've fallen into a crevasse or frozen to death on the surface—or, for that matter, if you've been poisoned by your Aunt Bertha—your body will at first sink ever more deeply into the ice, and then slowly rise back up to the surface, all the while inching downhill toward the valley. On the other hand, if you fall into a crevasse in the ablation zone, you won't sink at all, but only rise toward the surface as you travel toward the glacier's tongue. And if you freeze to death on the glacier's surface in the ablation zone, you'll stay on top and simply coast on down.

In 2012 a group of British climbers found three skeletons on the lower reaches of the Aletsch glacier. They were identified as a group of Swiss men from Valais who had gone missing in 1926. The reason they were skeletons and not mummies or large bars of soap was that they had surfaced some years before they were found, and either been picked clean, or rotted, or both. But these skeletons were not only clean; the bones in them were badly warped. Which leads us to another possibility for an icy corpse.

A team of glaciologists from the Federal Institute of Technology in Zurich tried to figure out where and how these climbers had died. To do this they used complex mathematical models to compute the trajectory of the corpses down the glacier—working backwards from the spot at which they had emerged.

The map below shows the course the scientists computed the bodies to have traveled. They must have entered the glacier somewhere in the rectangle on the left. By 1980 they had reached the Konkordiaplatz, at which point they had traveled about six kilometers horizontally and sunk to 250 meters below the surface of the ice. At this depth their bodies were subject to pressures some 25 times that of our normal atmosphere—and this is why their bones warped.

By now they had reached the ablation zone, so they moved ever closer to the surface over the last four kilometers of their journey, and finally broke out of their icy prison into daylight. Overall they traveled some 10.5 horizontal kilometers and 800 vertical meters over the course of 86 years.

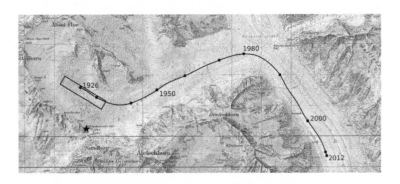

On August 15th, 1942, a 40-year-old shoemaker named Marcelin Dumoulin and his 37-year-old wife Francine, a teacher, left their seven children behind in the village of Chandolin in Valais to walk up to the alp where their cows were spending the summer. They didn't come back. The entire village searched for two and a half months—to no avail. But the couple wasn't lost forever. 75 years after their disappearance, on the 13th of July, 2017, they were released from the Tsanfleuron Glacier—hobnailed boots, wine bottle, rucksack and all. They were taken from the ice and buried in the church where they had married. Their youngest daughter, who was four when they disappeared, was seventy-nine when they showed up again. "I feel a true inner peace," she said, after finally experiencing her parents' funeral and a sense of closure about their death.

As global warming accelerates the melting of the glaciers, Swiss police expect many more pairs of hobnailed boots to emerge from the ice, allowing them to finally close hundreds of missing-persons cases unresolved for decades, or even centuries (see Question 32). In the Valaisan Alps alone, 135 persons have gone missing since 1925.

6

What Happens to All the Cow Manure?

Switzerland doesn't have *that* many cows.[1] Its human population of over 8 million well outnumbers its 1.5 million cattle, making about one cow for every five people. This is a lower cow to human ratio than, say, in the United States, far lower than in Brazil—where there are more cows than people—and about the same as in the country with more cattle than any other: (surprise!) India.[2] Most Swiss cows are semi-nomadic, in that they spend the winter in stalls at lower altitudes, the spring and summer at the *Maiensässe* halfway up a mountain, and the summer months up on the alp, or high pasture.[3]

The manure excreted in the summer, when the cows are outside most of the time, lands on the alp, and stays there, eventually decomposing and enriching the soil. This enrich-

---

1   Let's use cow in the colloquial sense meaning any kind of domestic cattle. Technically, a cow is a mature female member of the genus Bos. For that matter, a cow is a mature female seal, elk, walrus, moose, camel, hippopotamus, dolphin, whale, elephant, and god knows what else.

2   With about 30 million head of cattle, India is home to almost a third of the world's bovine population.

3   Alp means high pasture. The Alps are full of alps, but are not alps themselves: alps are alps, and Alps are a mountain range.

ment gets rather too strong in the areas around fountains and stalls, which turn into uninviting wastelands of dock and nettles. Even after an alp has been abandoned, these plants continue to block out the natural vegetation for decades. Elsewhere on the alp, where the concentration of waste is lower and the ground less mucky, single cow pies dry out and turn hard. They can be used to make a fire in a pinch. After the first frost they provide a growing medium for hallucinogenic mushrooms, which are collected by those in the know.

Meanwhile, back at the *Maiensäss*—the halfway house for cows—pies also drop onto the pastures, but the cows are likely to spend more time in the stall. If you return to a given barn every so often, you'll see a pile of manure mixed with straw bedding rising just outside it, and this relatively solid mix is later scattered into the fields in lumps by a vehicle brilliantly designed for that purpose.

The really bad shit happens down in the valley during the long winters. Here the manure and urine collect in a (usually underground) tank and ferment during the dark months of the year. Come spring, this makes a heady mixture. Called *Gül* in Swiss German, it's what the English call slurry, and it's not only stinky but dangerous. It needs to be stirred to thoroughly liquify it, and the fumes released while stirring are enough to kill a cow—or seven, as happened at one Swiss farm in 2013. Even rugby stars are not immune—the Irish Union player Nevin Spence, his father and his brother succumbed to the fumes and died in 2012 on their farm in Hillsborough. The culprit gas is hydrogen sulfate (though it's not the only nasty in the mix), which stinks terribly but employs the sly trick of knocking out your sense of smell after a whiff or two. Heavier than air, it settles above the mixing tank and kills more quickly than cyanide.

Once mixed, *Gül* is sprayed onto the pastures and hayfields in early spring, causing a stink that permeates whole villages for days at a time. In the process significant quantities of ammoniac, a powerful air pollutant, are released, in addition to two of the most potent greenhouse gases—methane and nitrous oxide—which damage the ozone layer and have a far stronger effect on climate than CO_2. Kilo for kilo, methane traps 25 times as much radiation as carbon dioxide over a 100-year period—and nitrous oxide is twelve times worse than methane.

But what happens to the air is only half the story. On the ground, the pasture turns a bright, lush green. This rich grass significantly ups milk production. Unfortunately, other forms of plant and animal life don't fare as well as the milk. Except for yellow springtime splashes of dandelions and buttercups, these meadows are almost exclusively green—the rich alpine flora has been killed off by the overwhelming power of the *Gül.* And with the flowers go the insects, and with the insects the small vertebrates and birds. *Gül* is thus responsible for a terrible loss of biodiversity in Swiss meadows—so much so that the government pays farmers *not* to spray it. The richly diverse unsprayed meadows, feasts of color and small creatures, are paradoxically called *Magerwiesen* in German— "skinny" meadows—as opposed to the "fat" meadows super-charged by *Gül.*[4]

But we're not finished yet. All that *Gül* deposits far too much nitrogen in the soil—60 percent more than it can handle, according to government studies—and from the ground the nitrogen ends up in the water. Some 45 percent of streams and

---

4   That rich biodiversity earns the appellation "skinny" while grass and dandelions get called "fat" might seem contradictory, but I guess it has to do with all that creamy milk.

ponds on Swiss agricultural land contain more than the permitted maximum level of nitrates, and this kills both water life and birds.

Gül, regular manure, and cows' flatulence and belching together make up the number one source of methane and nitrous oxide released into Swiss air, and Swiss agriculture overall produces—again according to government studies—over one-fourth of the greenhouse gases released in the entire country. This *may not even be the half of it, though.* A dispute rages over how to measure the contribution of cattle to climate change, and the real figure may be much higher.[5]

This may all seem a very pessimistic view of Swiss animal agriculture, and maybe you didn't really want to know what all those gentle animals in those peaceful, lush green pastures are doing to the land, water, air, and climate. Compared to factory farms in most of the rest of the world, Swiss farms are small, family-run, humane, and largely self-sufficient.[6] They are probably more respectful of animal welfare and less damaging to the environment than the farms of almost any other country.

But good for the planet they are not.

---

5   51 percent worldwide, according to a study by two World Bank analysts. See Goodland and Anhang, "Livestock and Climate Change" at http://www.worldwatch .org/files/pdf/Livestock%20and%20Climate%20Change.pdf.
6   80 percent of all farm workers are family members; Swiss animal protection laws are among the world's most stringent; and only about 20 percent of animal feed is imported.

7

Has Switzerland Ever Had a King or Queen?

No, but it has a sovereign.[1]

Switzerland's sovereign has close to absolute power. She can cancel at will any law passed by parliament and she can alter the Swiss constitution any time she pleases. In 2009 she arbitrarily and highhandedly decided, against the overwhelming advice of the executive and legislative officeholders of the Swiss government, to *forbid the building of a certain type of tower.* In 2012 she changed the constitution again and forbid the construction of a vast number of holiday homes. In 1992 the sovereign made one of her most sweeping and consequential decisions, shocking the elected political establishment: she canceled Switzerland's fledgling membership in the European Economic Area, and thus, effectively, its entrance to the EU.

The Federal Council—the highest executive in the land—and the Parliament—the elected legislature—can do nothing against the merciless and unpredictable will of this sovereign. She has forbidden the enlargement of the transit capacity of

---

1   The dictionary definition of sovereign is "a monarch: a king, queen, or other supreme ruler." Read on.

Alpine roads, has insisted that freight travel the country on trains rather than trucks, and has prohibited agriculture with genetically modified plants or animals. She has done all of this *against the strong recommendation* of the elected Swiss government.

On the day following each of these, and many other decisions, the newspapers regularly report that "The sovereign has decided . . ." (*Der Souverän hat entschieden . . .*).

Despite the despotic and arbitrary nature of their sovereign, and her almost unlimited power, the Swiss people have more confidence in their government than the people of any other country. A survey of 40 rich nations by the Organization for Economic Cooperation and Development in 2015 found that, on average, 42 percent of citizens expressed confidence in their government. Switzerland won first place in the survey, with, at 75 percent, a confidence level almost double the average.

This is because, in Switzerland, the sovereign is the people—to be more specific, those Swiss citizens who are of sound mind and voting age. It is the Swiss people who have the powers I have described above, and it is the Swiss people who made the decisions I have selected, ignoring the express wishes of their government in every case.

The English environmentalist and political commentator George Monbiot writes:

These [Swiss] procedures horrify many onlookers. They argue that they are likely to lead to instability, extremism, the oppression of minorities by majorities, and the rule of ignorance and stupidity.[2]

---

2   Monbiot is reporting here—he himself has a generally positive attitude toward the Swiss system.

But Switzerland is hardly unstable or extremist—quite the opposite. And if the rule of ignorance and stupidity leads to topping the Global Innovation Index for seven years running, to the most patents applied for and attained per capita (by far), and to the greatest wealth per person in the world, then maybe it's not such a bad thing—but maybe this isn't, after all, the rule of ignorance and stupidity.[3]

Most democracies are indirect: the people elect representatives, and the representatives make decisions for them. Swiss democracy is half-indirect, and half-direct. The Swiss people elect representatives, as it were, to *suggest* decisions to them—but the people get the final say. And when the representatives don't suggest the right kind of decisions, the people can suggest them themselves.

In order to challenge a law passed by parliament in a *referendum*, citizens have to collect 50,000 signatures and deliver them to the Federal Chancellery. Those 50,000 signatures represent less than one percent of eligible voters. Thus if even 1 out of 100 Swiss voters is willing to sign his or her name to a piece of paper, the whole legislative machinery of the country is blocked until every single voter has been asked for his or her opinion. While George Monbiot cited worries about the majority oppressing the minority, in fact it is a tiny minority of citizens that has an inordinate influence over the whole country.

---

3   On the other hand, it sometimes is. The "certain type of tower" forbidden by the 2009 vote is a minaret. Racist, Nazi-inspired posters—which were banned in Basel and Lausanne—incited to a prohibition about which the Federal Council had written: *A ban would violate many fundamental rights that are anchored in the Swiss constitution; it would also be a violation of human rights. Far from contributing to the protection of our civil structures, it would endanger religious peace in our country.*

Swiss voters don't only have the final say on laws passed by Parliament. They can also effect change by amending the constitution.[4] When Switzerland finally joined the UN in 2002, for example, it was not based on a change in government policy, but on a successful *popular initiative*. It takes only 100,000 signatures—representing less than 2 percent of Swiss voters—to bring such a proposal to the ballot box. This particular one earned 54 percent of the vote, and Switzerland became the 190th member of the United Nations. A tiny fraction of the population had thereby altered decades of the foreign policy practice of a modern nation-state.

The dark side to this power is, as one might expect, money. There are no limits to political funding or spending in Switzerland—including on referendums and popular initiatives—and no transparency either. Switzerland ranks at the bottom of the 47 member-states of the Council of Europe in this regard. Since 2011, the anti-corruption organization of the Council of Europe, GRECO, has chastised Switzerland four times for its lack of transparency, demanding the enactment of laws to regulate political spending—all in vain.[5] GRECO has now opened a non-compliance proceeding against Switzerland. The OECD has also condemned the Swiss practices—or lack thereof.

Far from considering GRECO's demands, however, the Swiss Federal Council has explicitly rejected them, claiming that financial transparency is not compatible with direct

---

4   For a popular initiative to pass, it must win not only a majority of the popular vote; a majority of the cantons must also vote for it.
5   GRECO stands for *Groupe d'Etats contre le corruption*, the Group of States Against Corruption.

democracy and other particularities of the Swiss political system. In 2014, all Swiss political parties except the Social Democrats rejected a proposal for even voluntary publishing of their financing. The Swiss Parliament has also repeatedly rejected proposals for laws to increase transparency.

Help may be on the way, however—from the implacable Swiss sovereign. On October 11th, 2017, a popular initiative "for greater transparency in political financing" was submitted to the Federal Chancellery by six parties, including the Pirate Party. The Chancellery has confirmed that 109,826 signatures were legitimately collected, meaning that there will be a vote at a still unspecified future date. The Federal Council has already recommended rejecting the initiative, and we can be sure that a great deal of anonymous and untraceable money will be poured into the campaign against it from the coffers of those who oppose transparency—perhaps, however, for the last time.

8

Who's the Fastest Climber in the Swiss Alps?

In 1938 the North Face of the Eiger—the "last unsolved problem in the Alps"—was finally climbed, after notoriously claiming many young men's lives. It took 85 hours for Anderl Heckmair, Fritz Kasparek, Ludwig Vörg and Heinrich Harrer to reach the summit.

In 1950 Leo Forstenlechner and Erich Wascak climbed the face in less than 24 hours, bivouacking on the mountaintop.

In 1963 the French climber Michel Darbellay climbed the face solo in 18 hours.

In 1974 Reinhold Messner and Peter Habeler made it up in 10.

In 1981 the Swiss guide Ueli Bühler cut it down to 8 hours and 30 minutes.

In 1982 the Slovene Farncek Knev did it in 6 hours.

In 1983 the Austrian Thomas Bubendorfer took only 4 hours and 50 minutes.

In 2003 Christoph Hainz broke Bubendorfer's record by 10 minutes.

In 2007 the Swiss speed climber Ueli Steck soloed the face in 3 hours 54 minutes. The following year Steck made that 2:47:33.[1]

In 2011 the Swiss guide Dani Arnold broke Steck's record, clocking 2:28. Arnold used fixed ropes that had been left on the face by previous climbers, while Steck had not.

In 2015 Steck, denying that there was any competition between him and Arnold, set the current (as of 2018) record of 2:22:50.7.[2]

Steck's achievement is mind-boggling. The Eiger North Face is a Grade VI climb of some 1,800 vertical meters in mixed rock and ice. It was considered unclimbable, even by the best alpinists in the world, in the 1930s. Steck danced up it at an average rate of 755 vertical meters per hour.

On October 21st, 2017, the Italian Philip Goetsch set a world record at the vertical kilometer race in Fully, Switzerland, completing a run with a 1,000 meter altitude difference in 28 minutes and 53 seconds—for an average speed of 2,077 vertical meters per hour. This is a guy who's wearing running shoes, lightweight shorts and a tank top while sprinting up the *steps* within a disused funicular track. He's pacing himself to do the kilometer as fast as possible, after which he is exhausted. Steck put in almost twice as many vertical meters, in climbing gear, pulling himself up with ice axes, scraping up via tiny toe-holds for his crampon points in loose, truly vertical rock and ice— at an average speed close to half of Goetsch's all-out run.

Although it really shouldn't come as a surprise when an extreme solo climber perishes in the mountains, it was for many

---

1   Yes, we're now measuring seconds.
2   Yes, we're now measuring tenths of seconds.

incomprehensible when Ueli Steck died on a training tour in the Himalaya on April 30th, 2017. Dominik Osswald wrote in the *Tagesanzeiger*:

Ueli Steck and death—those were two words which were often said together, and yet they seemed so distant from each other. He would always slip away. As if death were a figure on the hunt and Steck his shadow, always rushing just ahead of him. Looked at soberly, this was nonsense—no one is superhuman. And yet the news hit us like a wrecking ball in the face . . .

Steck was more than a climber. He was a researcher who ventured into the space between life and death and reported back to us stay-at-homes from a zone that no scientist with measurements and logic can approach . . . The other side waits for all of us, and nothing interests us with a more burning intensity than when a person finds an approach to risk and death, and can put this approach into words. Ueli Steck, the carpenter from Ringgenberg, could do that like no one else could.

Steck's death would seem to leave Dani Arnold as the fastest living climber, if the Eiger North Face is to be our standard.

If not, we might look at the Matterhorn. In 2013 the Catalan mountain runner Kilian Jornet *ran* up the Matterhorn—in running shoes, shorts, and a t-shirt. He overcame almost 2,500 vertical meters in 1:56:15, for an average vertical speed of some 1,275 meters per hour. This is faster than Steck or Arnold on the Eiger, but slower than Goetsch in Fully—and raises the question of whether it was a climb or a run. It seems to be something in between. In any event, the route Jornet took up the Matterhorn's southwest ridge isn't remotely comparable to the Eiger North Face—which we can safely say will never be dashed up in shorts and running shoes.

In the end, however, none of these humans even comes close to that superlative Alpine climber whose ease and beauty ascending and descending seemingly impossible rock faces strike us with awe. The chamois, *rupicapra rupicapra*, leaves humans in the dust. With a heart twice as large as ours in relation to its body size, exceptionally large lungs, and an enormous number of red blood cells for an ungulate, chamois have been observed to lay back 1,000 vertical meters in a few minutes without even getting out of breath. The Swiss naturalist Bertrand Gentizon timed a chamois in the Vallon des Morteys as it dashed up 300 vertical meters in a mere 1 minute and 45 seconds, for an average vertical speed of 10,285 meters per hour—about 5 times as fast as Goetsch on his run up the steps in Fully.

If a chamois were to keep up this speed, it would make Jornet's 2-hour run up the Matterhorn in less than 15 minutes.

9

Will Geneva Vanish In a Black Hole?

Geneva is home to CERN, the lab running the world's largest particle accelerator, or, as CERN puts it, "the world's largest and most complex scientific instruments, [used] to probe the fundamental structure of the universe." The pearl of CERN is the Large Hadron Collider, or LHC, in which tiny particles are accelerated to almost the speed of light and then smashed into each other. The LHC is 27 kilometers in circumference, and most of it is in France. It's not really *in* France, though, but 175 meters *under* France. The part of it that's in—well, *under*—Switzerland, scoots along just north of Geneva's airport.

When the LHC began operations, the online bookmaker William Hill offered odds of 666,666,666:1 on a bet that a CERN-induced black hole would swallow up the world. This sounds relatively safe—there are quite a few digits in that number—until you realize that the odds were set by the bettor, not the bookie. As one employee chortled at the time,

We are more than happy to offer whatever odds punters would like on the end of the world happening; and should

the worst prediction be proved correct, at least your last thoughts can be that you are extremely rich.

If we can't rely on William Hill to lay the odds on an LHC black hole, who can we rely on? Perhaps CERN itself? Here's CERN's take on the matter [sic]:

The creation of black holes at the Large Hadron Collider is very unlikely. However, some theories suggest that the formation of tiny 'quantum' black holes may be possible.

But isn't a "tiny black hole" like "a little bit pregnant?" Astrophysicist George Greenstein has described what might happen if a fairly small hole—say, one foot in diameter—were to appear in your bedroom. You could push various objects into it—a yardstick, a sofa, rotting garbage—and all would disappear without a trace, a sound, a smell. You might throw in a hand grenade about to detonate—the hole wouldn't even quiver. You could throw in a hydrogen bomb with the same effect.

Of course, you wouldn't be able to do these things, as you would yourself have immediately been sucked into the hole and disappeared. So would your house, and so would the entire atmosphere of the earth. So would Lake Geneva, the Mediterranean, the Atlantic and Indian and Pacific Oceans—every drop of them. So would Geneva's airport, and the rest of Geneva, and Basel, and Los Angeles. In fact, to cut to the chase, so would the entire planet Earth. Not instantaneously, as there would be the mother of all traffic jams as everything tried to get *into* the hole. The traffic would quickly diminish, however, as the rubble was swallowed—now a kilometer across, now a meter. And then it is gone. Greenstein writes:

Finally, only the hole remains. It does not quiver. Only one minor change has taken place. Because the hole has absorbed so much mass, it has grown a little heavier. The Schwarzschild radius is then a little bigger. The mouth grows as it devours.

It is this "growing" that might make the "tiny" black holes in Geneva seem worrying.

But maybe not, after all. CERN would like to set our minds at ease: "The observation of such an event [a black hole] would be thrilling in terms of our understanding of the universe; it would also be perfectly safe."

Unfortunately, the words "Don't worry, it's perfectly safe" are not, to my mind, extremely reassuring. It's the kind of thing someone says when they're drunk and sitting behind the wheel of a car. It's what you hear just before a bungee jump that doesn't end well.

And yet, we may have no choice but to simply put our faith in CERN's assurances—much as you do in those of the dude who ties you to the bungee cord. After all, who knows more about micro-black holes than the thousands of very smart scientists who work at the world's biggest lab—one of whom, in case you're doubting their smarts, invented the little thing we call the Internet?[1] And these very smart people tell us that, if one of these micro-black holes were to be created in the LHC, it would "evaporate" in a very short time: 10^{-25} seconds. This is many *septillion* times quicker than the blink

---

1   Actually the World Wide Web. The Internet is a set of connected hardware and was created in the 1960s by the US military in order to maintain communications in the event of a nuclear war. The Web is the information *on* the Internet and consists of pages that can be viewed with a web browser. The Web was invented in 1989 by Tim Berners-Lee at CERN.

of an eye. (Coincidentally, if you were smushed into a ball with radius 10^{-25} *meters*, you'd become a black hole yourself.)

So the next time you're landing at Geneva's Cointrin Airport, and contemplating the Large Hadron Collider's proximity to the runway, just think to yourself: I can trust the people at CERN—the *E*uropean *L*aboratory for *P*article *P*hysics. True, they're pretty bad at acronyms, but maybe that's because they're such brilliant, absent-minded scientists.

Actually, forget I said "absent-minded." Just . . . brilliant scientists.[2]

---

2   CERN was a good acronym back when it referred to the *Conseil Européene pour Recherche Nucleaire*—an organization that was disbanded in 1954. Since then it's been doing less well. CERN doesn't even do nuclear research anymore, but rather particle physics—which is a different kettle of fish. Thus it is most commonly referred to as the European Laboratory for Particle Physics. Werner Heisenberg, author of the Uncertainty Principle, is (appropriately) credited with advocating that CERN be kept as an acronym, even when it no longer was. We might dub this the UnCERNtainty Principle.

10

Am I More Likely to be the Victim of a Mass Shooting in Switzerland, or in the USA?

On September 27, 2001, Friedrich Leibacher entered the Parliament building in Canton Zug and shot to death 14 politicians with four different guns. He fired 91 rounds, wounding eleven people besides those who died, set off a homemade bomb, and then shot himself. He acted in the belief that he was being persecuted by the cantonal authorities, and left a letter behind entitled "Day of Wrath for the Zug Mafia."

Due solely to this incident, the death rate by mass shooting between 2000 and 2014 was 1.7 per million people in Switzerland. In the United States, by contrast, there were 133 mass shootings in the same period of time—for a death rate of 1.5 per million. Had Switzerland had as low a rate during these years as the United States, only 12.4 politicians would have died on the Day of Wrath in Zug.

You might object that mass shootings are an anomaly in Switzerland, and that the high toll of this single incident and the small population of the country combine to render this statistic meaningless. In the United States, you might say, mass shootings are a regular enough occurrence that the numbers actually mean something.

Before dismissing the statistic entirely, however, it's worth putting it into a relevant context. A recent study by University of Alabama professor Adam Lankdorf demonstrates that mass shootings, both internationally and locally, are correlated with only one single variable. This variable is not mental health, it is not the playing of video games, it is not racial diversity, and it is not overall crime rate. It is, purely and simply, the rate of gun ownership.

And Switzerland has, after the United States, the highest rate of gun ownership among all developed countries. Its gun homicide rate—in 2004, 7.7 deaths per million people—is correspondingly very high. The rate in Great Britain is eleven times lower.

If Lankdorf's conclusion is correct, we can *expect* Switzerland to have an exceptionally high rate of deaths by mass shooting. It ought not to be higher than that of the United States—as it was in the period from 2000 to 2014—but rather, based on gun ownership statistics, about half as high: the second highest in the developed world. Thus, while the Zug massacre was horrifying and shocking, it can't truly be said to be an anomaly.

As, indeed, it wasn't. In 1912 in Romanshorn a local man began shooting from the window of his house. He hit twelve people and killed six on the spot.

This is probably not the result the Swiss Tourism Office is looking for. But, as the comedian Eddie Izzard has commented, spoofing the slogan of the National Rifle Association: "Guns don't kill people. People kill people. (Pause) But I think the gun *helps.*"

Swiss guns *help* just as much as their American cousins.

11

Did William Tell Really Shoot an Apple Off His Son's Head?

Before we get into this, it's worth noting that it's a deeply fraught question in Switzerland. One agnostic observer writes:

> *If one examines the fierce and emotional battles of faith that have been fought over the past 200 years and are still being fought today over the existence or non-existence of William Tell, one cannot avoid designating the question of the existence of William Tell* as a religious question, *concerning which not a few intellectuals argue more from their gut than from provable facts.*

If not a religious question, at least it's a political one. A 2017 survey by the research institute Sotomo found that some 40 percent of members of the right-wing Swiss People's Party (SVP) believed in the historical Tell, as against only 6 percent of people on the left. Meanwhile, in a 2018 Sotomo poll, the Swiss chose Tell as history's second most courageous figure—

a couple of points behind Nelson Mandela, but ahead of number three, Mahatma Gandhi, and number four, Swiss climber Ueli Steck (see Question 8). Jesus Christ placed tenth in the survey, with a percentage less than a third of Tell's.

The potency of the Tell symbolism is not lost on Switzerland's gun lobby: the Swiss version of the NRA calls itself Pro Tell, and currently advocates abandoning all bilateral treaties with the EU rather than conforming to new EU regulations limiting private ownership of semi-automatic weapons (see Question 10). A referendum to this effect is being readied as I write (see Question 7).

According to the historian André Holenstein, the Tell myth bloomed in the 19th and early 20th centuries, when, as a newly constituted and internally diverse nation, Switzerland was surrounded by enemies and needed a powerful legend to justify its existence. Yet the Tell story was clearly sacred even before then. When the 18th century Bernese scholar Gottlieb von Haller dared to question its authenticity in a book entitled *William Tell: a Danish Fable*, he earned himself a court battle, a book burning in the Altdorf town square, and, but that he abjectly recanted—explaining that his work was a mere "literary exercise," and not meant to be taken seriously—he might have been burned at the stake himself.

The story matters, then, in more than academic terms. Here it is:

> *The tyrant said, "I will now place an apple on the head of your little son and you will shoot it off." T. took up his weapon, placed an arrow inside his jacket, aimed a second arrow at his son, fired, and split the apple. The tyrant then said, "Why did you put the other arrow in your jacket?"*

T. answered him: "To kill you with, had my first shot killed my son." T. later ambushed the tyrant and put an arrow through his heart.

That, in a nutshell, is the story of William Tell—down to the small details, like the second arrow in the jacket and the wonderful response to the question about what it was for. The problem is that this story doesn't come from Switzerland. It comes from a 12th century chronicle called *Gesta Danorum* that was written by Saxo Grammaticus—in Denmark. The T. in the story isn't Tell; he's a Viking named Toko. And the story took place several centuries before Tell was supposedly born.

If that weren't enough, in the Old Norse *Thidriksaga* the tale appears again. This time the son is three years old, and the hero puts away *two* arrows for the worst case. And in the *Malleus Maleficarum,* a fifteenth century Latin work justifying the persecution of witches, the hero goes us one better: he shoots a coin off his son's head.

How the Danish tale got transferred to Uri is anyone's guess, but it could have been via pilgrims crossing the St. Gotthard on their way to Rome. Sitting around in a pub one night, the Danes tell their Viking story to some local folk. It perfectly exemplifies the qualities of a freedom fighter, and the locals attach it at the next telling to one of their own.

Whether there was a real folk hero named Tell, to whom the legend got attached, is also anybody's guess—but since the legend is all we know of Tell, it's kind of a moot point. There is in any event no evidence for any Tell, though there is a Thall who appears in 1472 in a manuscript called the *White Book of Sarnen.* This is more than a century and a half after our hero is supposed to have left his mark, however, so any resemblance may be purely coincidental.

*   *   *

Whether the Viking Toko actually existed, and shot an apple off of *his* son's head, is also undiscoverable. There is in fact only one Tell act that we know to have occurred, and it happened in Mexico, and it didn't end well. William Burroughs, the American Beat poet, artist, and heroin addict, took his handgun from his bag in a Mexico City bar and announced to his wife that "It's time for our William Tell act." She balanced a highball glass on her head. Burroughs aimed, fired, missed, and blew her brains out.

12

What Did the Swiss Alps Look Like to the Dinosaurs?

In 2015 the headless skeleton of an 8-meter-long Plateosaurus was dug up in Frick, Canton Aargau. When this giant lizard roamed his boggy territory, he could look long and far without seeing a single hill. The land around him was flat, very hot, and crisscrossed with rivers. He probably got stuck in the boggy earth and died of thirst. His splayed legs suggest as much, as do the many other finds of detached dinosaur legs in the area. These dinosaurs sank to the hips in the mucky ground and died. Their legs became fossilized remains; the upper body, above the muck, rotted away.

Imagine weighing three and a half tons and getting stuck in the mud.

It happened a lot. Paleontologists hypothesize that whole troops of dinosaurs may have perished like this around Frick. The site is world-renowned for the density of its dinosaur remains. Within a diameter of 3 kilometers an average of 500 dinosaurs have been found per hectare—that's about one of the monsters for every 5 × 5 meter square! The area seems to have been particularly attractive to herbivores: only one meat-eater turns up for every hundred vegetarians.

Many four-year-olds will be able to tell you that the dinosaurs roamed the Earth in the Triassic, Jurassic and Cretaceous periods. Precocious ones will add that the asteroid that ended them smashed into the Yucatan 66 million years ago.[1]

Most will not be able to tell you, however, that the Alps only started to form 55 million years ago. This means that over 10 *million* years passed—about five *thousand* times as long as the span from Jesus of Nazareth to Donald Trump—between the last dinosaur and the first fold in the bed of the Tethys sea. Parts of that sea-bottom today jut into the air as Alpine peaks, but the Triassic Plateosaurus mentioned above—who was so large that the Frick Dinosaur Museum had to be extended to house him—missed the start of the mountain show by over 150 million years.

It's hard to believe, when you stand in front of that headless skeleton, that living beings could be so very much older than huge mountains. The eternal snows are hardly eternal; the dinosaurs are older than the hills.

---

1   Excepting the birds, who survived. Modern birds are a kind of dinosaur—the chicken, which is the most successful species of fowl ever to have existed in terms of numbers, is particularly close to the ancient monsters.

13

Who is Switzerland's Worst Arsonist?

On the night of the 11th of May, 1861, the city of Glarus—capital of the canton of the same name—went up in flames. The glow of the fire could be seen as far away as Basel and Ravensburg. Two-thirds of the buildings were destroyed and half the population was left homeless. The origin of the fire was hushed up for 150 years.

Only in 2011 was the truth uncovered, with journalist Walter Hauser's discovery of illuminating documents in the state archives in Bern and Rome. The documents show that two Swiss Catholics, Augusto Engeler and Ulrich Göldli, fled Switzerland after the Glarus fire and joined the Pope's Swiss Guard at the Vatican. In 1867 they abandoned the Pope's service and were arrested for desertion. While awaiting trial, Engeler was overheard boasting of having set the Glarus fire. Under interrogation, he and Göldli confessed to the arson. The Swiss Federal Council requested their extradition, but the Pope's right-hand man, Cardinal Antonelli, feared a scandal, and instead sent the men off to sea—as oarsmen on a galley. Engeler died in 1871, at 26 years of age. Of Göldli there are no further records.

The Glarus fire was the most devastating conflagration in Swiss history. But it wasn't in fact all Engeler's and Göldli's doing. There was another actor involved. And on August 18th, 1892, he sprang into action again—in Grindelwald. The Slovenian alpinist Julius Kugy happened to be approaching the town on that day and wrote this description of what he saw:

Great clouds of smoke were rising from the Grindelwald valley. I thought it must be a forest fire, while Kaufmann took it for dust from paths and moraines. When we reached the Bäregg, we saw what it was: Grindelwald was on fire! . . . Houses, hotels, railway station, wagons, hay-sheds, fences, cornfields, telegraph-poles, all were ablaze . . . Kaufmann saw his house threatened, but still standing. His money was inside. We raced down, but by the time we were below, his house was a smoldering ruin. He took his place calmly at the fire-hose, while Bonetti and I labored the whole afternoon, and throughout the night till next dawn, in the water-chain. British ladies stood side by side with the native inhabitants, passing the buckets. Purtscheller and Blodig had bravely rescued a piano and an omnibus, but these two valuable articles each started a fire to themselves later on . . .

The English ski pioneer Arnold Lunn also happened to be in town, and later wrote: "I can still shut my eyes and see the Eiger snows blood-red in the glare reflected from the flames which consumed the greater part of Grindelwald."

In 1879 and 1891, Meiringen had been similarly laid waste, and by the same arsonist. In the latter fire 176 houses were turned to ashes and 792 people were left without homes.

It's hard to get an exact fix on our arsonist's place of origin—some claim he was the oldest inhabitant of Grindelwald, some say of the Hasli valley, where he has been more active. Besides the two conflagrations in Meiringen, he burned down the Hasli village of Guttannen in its entirety three times. His age is also impossible to fix—while he performed his evil work on human habitations for centuries, he is known to have lived and worked long before human beings ever arrived on the territory that is now Switzerland. We have given him a name, however: Föhn.

The Föhn is a powerful wind that blows when air pressure north of the Alps is significantly lower than the pressure in the south. Moist air, heading north, rises as it hits the south side of the mountains, cools, condenses, and rains or snows heavily. By the time it has crossed the Alps it is exceptionally dry; and since dry air heats up quickly as it loses altitude, it gets unusually warm as it shoots down the northern mountain slopes. Temperatures of 20 degrees Celsius are common even in midwinter.

Like water, air seeks the lowest spots to cross a barrier. In this case the barrier is the Alps, and one of the lowest spots is the Grimsel pass, at the head of the long Hasli valley—into which the wind is funneled and accelerated by the "jet-effect," just as water accelerates when a river narrows. Gusts of well over 100 kilometers per hour are a common occurrence in Meiringen during Föhn.

The Föhn valleys have special watches that patrol for the first sign of fire. In Guttannen, the watch patrols from 10 at night until 4 in the morning, when the farmers rise to milk their cows. It is authorized to enter any house in the village, if, for example, a spark is seen exiting a chimney.[1]

---

1   This is easy to do in Guttannen, where doors are seldom locked.

Cigarette smoking anywhere outside is strictly forbidden when the Föhn is blowing, as is any sort of outdoor fire. As late as the 1960s a Meiringen law forbade even the baking of bread during Föhn. A student at a Hasliberg boarding school wrote of the consequences in 1964: "As the wind continued to howl, we were served stale bread, and eventually, no bread at all."

14

Why Aren't There "No Trespassing" Signs on Privately Owned Swiss Land?

On the 18th of May, 2011, a man referred to in public court documents as "X" was leading a gold-panning course.[1,2] To get to the stream in the woods where he intended to pan for gold, his group had to walk along a dirt road between two meadows. This area, however, was fenced in with an electric fence, and the dirt road was blocked by a locked gate. A judicial order hung on the gate forbidding entry.

X unscrewed two insulators and cut through the fence wire with a hammer. He then led his course along the dirt road through the meadows and into the woods to the stream.

---

1   Yes, a gold panning course.
2   Gold panning is "Goldwaschen" in German, and is a legal activity. Not to be confused with "Geldwaschen," which means money laundering and is illegal—unless you do it with very expensive lawyers (see Question 37).

A farmer referred to as "A" charged X with violating the judicial order, crossing his private land, and damaging his property.

In 2015 the case reached the Swiss Supreme Court.

The section of the Swiss Law Book relevant to the case is Article 699, a single, almost sacred sentence with profound and far-reaching effects. Here it is:

Access on foot to forests and pastures and the collecting of wild berries, mushrooms and so on are allowed to every person, as long as the relevant authorities have not issued particular and limited prohibitions in order to protect crop production.

In the case of A versus X, the relevant authorities had certainly issued a particular prohibition—the judicial order prohibiting "Trespassing" on the farmer's land. The Supreme Court ruled this order invalid: walking on a dirt road can in no way damage crop production. That the land belonged to A was irrelevant, because everyone has a right to walk through and forage in anyone else's forests and pastures, according to Article 699. The court found that X was acting fully within his rights in leading his group down the dirt road on A's property and searching for gold.[3]

This case highlights the fact that Switzerland has not allowed common land to be enclosed. In contrast, the "enclosures," a

---

3   It was not okay, however, for X to damage A's property. In a separate decision, the Supreme Court rejected X's appeal of a lower court decision that fined him for minor property damage. Rather than damaging A's property—which the court saw as an instance of vigilante justice—X should have gone to court in advance to demand the judicial order rescinded and the gate unlocked.

brutal and shattering series of episodes in British history (as elsewhere), at a stroke transformed commonly accessible land—the source of livelihood for millions of people—into private property protected by "No Trespassing" signs.[4] In the US and Australia colonists and then governments stole the forests and prairies and deserts and bush that had been the common resource of the Native Americans, the Aborigines and wild animals, and declared them the property of particular white men.[5] These tragic and arbitrary assertions of ownership of what had once been the common habitat and pantry both of human beings and animals are taken for granted almost everywhere today. Switzerland, along with Scotland and some Scandinavian countries, represent remarkable if partial holdouts against the "No Trespassing" mindset that defines much of today's world.

The far-reaching effects of Article 699 play into the impressions of the Swiss journalist Peter Sennhauser, who visited the United States—a country in which "No Trespassing" signs are endemic—in 2012.

Roads that dissolve on the horizon into endless distances. From here to that horizon, besides the road, no sign of

---

4   The so-called "Tragedy of the Commons," in which greedy individualists exploit common land to their own immediate advantage but ultimately to everyone's detriment, is an economist's myth designed to justify enclosures. In practice—as on Swiss alps and among many indigenous peoples—the commons are protected by self-regulation and the ostracization of those who act out of excessive self-interest. Among most indigenous peoples hoarding—being rich—brings low social status rather than, as in most of our societies, the opposite.

5   In 1988 the Australian Aborigine Burnum Burnum planted an Aboriginal flag on the cliffs of Dover and claimed Great Britain for the Australian Aborigines. Ha ha. But why Ha ha? Exactly two hundred years earlier Arthur Phillip of the British First Fleet had done exactly the same on Burnum Burnum's land—with far-reaching and disastrous consequences. (For Eddie Izzard on the clever use of flags in colonialism, see his *Dress to Kill*.)

human civilization. This simple knowledge slowly sinks into one's consciousness and creates the inexplicable feeling of freedom that we love to connect with America and the Wild West.

These expanses, however, have precious little to do with freedom. All along the road, for hundreds of miles, a parade of fences closes in the land. And on these fences are the signs: "No Trespassing," "Private Property," "Enter at Your Own Risk," "Intruders will be Shot without Warning." And the owners mean what they say.

If you're looking for the land of freedom, Sennhauser tells his Swiss readers, you won't find it across the ocean. It's right out your front door.

This doesn't mean you're free to blaze a trail across every grassy expanse in Switzerland, however. Article 699 refers to pastures, not meadows. While these two words are not completely distinct in everyone's mind—nor in every dictionary—a pasture is a place for animals to graze, and a meadow is a place to make hay. The surest way to rile up a Swiss farmer is to walk through a field of tall grass, trampling down a path and rendering this part of her "crop" unharvestable.

Of course, if you're looking at a nice green field of grass, it's sometimes hard to know if it's going to be used for cattle or haymaking, and one and the same field can alternately be used for both. Thus local regulations usually specify that fields of grass below the treeline can't be crossed between May 1st and October 1st unless they've been freshly mowed—with "freshly mowed" generally meaning that the grass is less than a fist high.

A freshly mowed field, however, is fair game. And not only as a place to walk, but as a place to *land* as well. Paragliders in Switzerland enjoy an astonishing freedom in where they can take off from (pretty much anywhere above the tree-line, and many places below) and where they can touch down (any mowed field).

The reason, then, that there are no "No Trespassing" signs in Switzerland is quite simple: trespassing is allowed. Even from the air.

15

Did Kim Jong-un Go to School in Switzerland?

From 1998 to 2000, a Korean boy named Pak-un, allegedly the son of a North Korean diplomat, attended the Liebefeld Steinitz school, a normal Swiss state school in Köniz, outside of Bern. He loved NBA basketball and Jackie Chan and James Bond movies. He lived on Kirchgasse 10—a residence belonging to the North Korean embassy—and often walked to school in the morning. In his first year he attended special classes to bring his German up to snuff. His desk-mate was a Portuguese boy, now a cook. Pak-un once showed this boy a photograph of himself at an official function, and confided that his father was the ruler of North Korea. In the autumn of 2000, he abruptly left school and returned to Pyongyang.

In a 1999 class photo taken at the Liebefeld Steinitz school, Pak-un stands in the back row. Enlarging his face and comparing the image to a photograph of Kim Jong-un from 2012, Raoul Perrot, a forensic anthropologist at the University of Lyon, determined that there is a 95 percent conformity between the two faces. He concluded that the two photos "most likely" depict the same person.

Over a decade after the photo was taken, a Swiss classmate remembered a visit to Pak-un's home at Kirchgasse 10:

I remember once, we were given some spaghetti to eat, and it was served rather cold, and he spoke to the servants in a manner that was quite sharp. I was surprised because it was not how he normally was.

The *Washington Post* reported that Kim Jong-un attended the International School of Bern under the name of Chol-pak or Pak-chol. A boy of such a name, who was thought to be the son of a North Korean embassy driver, is recorded as having attended that school from 1993 to 1998.

Digging further, however, we find our original Pak-un registered at the Hessgut school in Liebefeld in 1997—from where he advanced to its sister middle school, the Liebefeld Steinitz school, in '98. Even Kim Jong-un can't have been at two Swiss schools at the same time. Many people now think that the student at the International School of Bern was Kim Jong-un's older brother—the second of Kim Jong-il's three sons—Kim Jong-chol.

Meanwhile Kim Jong-un's aunt, Ko Yung-suk, claims that he lived with her family in Bern from 1996 onward.

We lived in a normal house and acted like a normal family. I acted like their mother. I encouraged him to bring his friends home, because we wanted them to live a normal life. I made snacks for the kids. They ate cake and played with Legos.

Other reports suggest that Ri Su-yung, who currently sits near Kim on the Politburo and previously served for 22 years as ambassador to Switzerland, was the young Kim's mentor in Bern. This may square with the fact that Ko Yong-suk and her husband defected to the US in 1998, where they underwent plastic surgery and were enrolled in the CIA's witness protection program. When Kim's mother heard about her sister's defection, she is said to have threatened to "track her down and make her pay, saying; 'How can she abandon the family and escape just for herself?'"

Putting it all together, the most likely scenario is that Kim Jong-un moved to Bern in 1996 and lived with his aunt, who was already taking care of his brother while *he* attended the International School of Bern. Kim enrolled at the Hessgut school in 1997 and learned German. In 1998 he moved up to the Liebefeld Steinitz school and his aunt defected, leaving him under the care of Ambassador Ri Su-yung. He remained in Bern until the autumn of 2000, when he was called back to Pyongyang.

The most mysterious part of this story is why Kim was enrolled in a typical Swiss state school, where he studied in German and would have spoken Swiss German on the playground. Why was he not at the International School of Bern like his older brother? Why were not both of them at a posh Swiss boarding school, like fellow dictator Mohammad Reza Pahlavi, the former Shah of Iran—who attended the world's allegedly most expensive school, Le Rosey? Perhaps the answer is that attending a perfectly unremarkable Swiss state school was the most inconspicuous way for a paranoid dictator's son to obtain an education.

In Edgar Allen Poe's "The Purloined Letter," detectives tear a hotel apart searching for secret crannies in which a stolen letter of great consequence must have been hidden. But the document was more cleverly hidden than in any secret cranny—it was openly hanging on a ribbon from a mantelpiece, along with a number of completely insignificant visiting cards. Kim Jong-un, similarly, walked, unremarked and unremarkable, to his Swiss state school every day—unnoticed, unsuspected, and completely exposed.

16

What are Switzerland's *Real* Traditional Foods?

Not Fondue, Rösti and Raclette.

Fondue as a national dish was invented in 1930 by the Swiss Cheese Union in order to sell cheese. The Union created pseudo-regional recipes, and promoted the dish as part of a "spiritual defense of Switzerland."

Melted cheese cooked with wine had been eaten sporadically before the Union got involved—a book published in Zurich in 1699 provides a recipe using the combination. It was only around 1875, however, that wealthy townspeople in the lowlands of French-speaking Switzerland began to eat our modern (traditional) version, and to name it "fondue" (which means melted). Before 1875, "fondue" referred to a cheese omelet. The association of fondue with mountain peasants is pure fiction: mountain peasants couldn't afford to eat the Gruyère cheese they produced, as it fetched too high a price as an export commodity.

Rösti—grated and fried potatoes—first appeared in 19th century Zurich as *brätlete Herdöpfel*—grilled potatoes. It spread to Canton Bern where it was christened *Rösti*—which means roasted—and became the favored morning meal of Bernese farmers, providing a welcome relief from the traditional porridges and mash. Today Rösti is more often served for lunch or dinner.

Today's raclette—cheese melted on boiled potatoes, with pickles, pickled onions, quartered tomatoes, pepper and Fendant wine—is equally an invention of the 20th century. Alpine peasants are mentioned melting cheese over fires as early as 1291 in Cantons Obwalden and Nidwalden, but they scraped the cheese onto bread. Melted cheese on bread later became a staple of Valaisan peasants, but it was known simply as roasted cheese. The name "raclette"—from the French *racler*, to scrape—is first attested in 1874. Today's dish and its national status are a result of clever marketing at the Cantonal Exhibition in Sion in 1909.

You may think that a hundred or so years is enough to justify a food as "traditional"—even if the tradition *was* created by clever marketing. I'd like to find some Swiss foods, however, with a somewhat longer pedigree.

Paleolithic hunter-gatherers, who lived on the small patch of Swiss tundra during the last ice age (see Question 48), primarily ate the meat of horses, reindeer, alpine hares and snow grouse, as well as the eggs of wild birds. The only one of these foods regularly eaten in Switzerland today is horsemeat, and I would suggest that this gives it a claim to represent the longest Swiss culinary tradition.

In the Mesolithic period the glaciers had retreated and the diet changed. The most consumed meats became red deer, boar, roe deer and beaver, and there is evidence that, besides meat, hazelnuts were the most important item in the diet. All of these foods except beaver are still consumed in Switzerland today.

By far the most frequently eaten meals from the beginning of Swiss agriculture some 7,000 years ago until quite recently, have probably been the poor peasant fare of wheat, millet or barley gruel with pulses like broadbeans and the odd green or bit of meat thrown in—rounded out with some cooked or dried fruit. South of the Alps chestnuts—often ground into flour—provided a significant source of calories. And bread, bread, bread.

In the Middle Ages the poor person's bread bore little resemblance to baguettes, croissants and brioches. It was a dense black rye and was communally baked in the mountain valleys *twice per year.* Nineteenth century tourists who broached remote Alpine areas often complained of it: the French novelist Alexandre Dumas described "a piece of alleged bread, hard and grey as a square inch of stone," while Leslie Stephen (see Question 32) spoke of "loaves whose consistency suggested that a Kippel father of a family would be doing a really humane action in giving his children stones for bread." These hard loaves, which remained edible (for peasants) for up to six months after their baking, were often rendered as payment for services in mountain economies that hardly knew of money (See Question 25).

Milk products were seldom consumed before the Late Middle Ages, and the animals kept in the mountains were, until then, almost exclusively sheep and goats. It was only with the opening of the Gotthard pass in the 13th century and an increasing demand for butter in Lombardy that mountain agriculture fully embraced dairy. The 15th century invention of hard cheeses, which could be stored for long periods, accelerated this trend. Still, it was not until the 1800s that the keeping of stock became the dominant mode of Swiss agriculture. For most of Swiss history, peasants owned but a few small animals, and, having little to feed them during the winter, slaughtered any excess in the autumn. This provided a bit of meat to add to gruel in the cold, dark months.

At the end of the 18th century new foods filtered in from the Americas, and new habits evolved. Potatoes, corn and coffee, previously unknown, became staples: breakfast in the Swiss plateau and Jura mountains was most often potatoes and coffee, with the potatoes often dipped into the coffee as we might dip a croissant. At the same time, in Ticino, St. Gallen and parts of Graubünden, polenta took its place as the morning (and evening) meal.

The wealthy, of course, had a more refined and varied diet. The French essayist Michel de Montaigne was in Basel in 1580, and describes how he was served.

> *As to the meat, they serve only two or three dishes thereof, cut in slices . . . A fresh dish is never served till the foregoing one shall have been finished. The valet . . . serves the fruit in two dishes all mixed together like the other courses. At this stage they often serve radishes, and with your roast meat you will most likely have been offered cooked pears. Amongst other edibles they give a high place to the crayfish, and honor it by serving it in a covered dish, a tribute they pay to hardly any other viand. The whole country abounds in these fish, and they are served every day, and rated as a delicacy.*

Putting this all together, I'm inclined to make an unorthodox list of traditional Swiss foods. From the stone age, I pick horsemeat and hazelnuts. From the peasants, I pick a millet and vegetable gruel, with some five-month-old black bread, and, to honor the Ticino, a few chestnuts. To mark the introduction of foods from the Americas, I'm going for potatoes dipped in coffee. And from the rich, I select the highly honored crayfish. Horsemeat, hazelnuts, gruel, black bread, chestnuts, coffee-dipped potatoes, and crayfish—these are traditional Swiss foods, without the marketing.

17

How Much Does Heroin Cost in Switzerland?

Nothing.

In the early 1990s Switzerland had a terrible heroin problem. Thousands of addicts took over the Platzspitz park next to the Swiss National Museum in central Zurich. When efforts at dispersing them only succeeded in shifting the problem elsewhere, Zurich decided it was better to contain the problem, and police were forbidden from entering the park or making arrests. Addicts shot up, OD'd nightly, overwhelmed the emergency services, and became infected with HIV; dealers fought violently for control over the market while users turned to crime to support their habits; the beautiful baroque park was ankle-deep in garbage and used needles. Even more shockingly, junkies parked themselves directly in front of the Federal Palace in Bern, seat of the Federal Council and the Parliament; politicians had to thread their way through trash, needles, and passed-out addicts to go to work. Switzerland was getting some very strange looks in the international press—the *New York Times* described the Zurich park as "a monument to vain utopian hope and sordid devastation."

Switzerland got even stranger looks for the bold move it took to address the problem: doctor-prescribed heroin, in a controlled setting, for severe addicts for whom other therapies had failed. The clean, government-inspected heroin that addicts receive today is produced in a lab in a large old house—the exact location is confidential—in the Bernese Oberland, and transported to distribution centers in handcuffed cases inside armored vehicles.

Today there is general agreement that the policy has worked. About 1,750 addicts take part in the program and, significantly, they are aging—heroin has become unattractive to young people. There are far fewer overdoses, less HIV transmission, and less crime committed to support drug habits. The health and social integration of the addicts has improved and public spaces are safer. The Federal Office of Health estimates that there are 1.7 drug deaths for every 100,000 Swiss residents. This compares very well with, say, the UK, where that number is 5.8, and phenomenally with the US, where, largely due to the current opioid crisis, the average across the entire country is 19.8 per 100,000 residents. This is over ten times the Swiss rate—and some states are doing significantly worse: West Virginia at 52, Ohio and New Hampshire at 39, and Pennsylvania at 38 per 100,000. If Switzerland had the same rate as West Virginia, over 4,000 more Swiss would die each year of overdoses.

This doesn't mean there's no illegal heroin scene in Switzerland, however. A 2017 study by the University of Lausanne estimates that there are over 12,000 regular and 10,000 occasional users of black market stuff. Among other methods, the study used sewage analysis to estimate the extent of drug use—Swiss sewage is laced not only with gold (see Question 4) but also with smack.[1]

The Lausanne report concludes that the illegal drug market in Switzerland is almost exclusively controlled by the Albanian mafia—but isn't very lucrative, as drug trades go. The price of heroin on the street has dropped from a high of 500 francs per gram in the 1980s to between 20 and 40 francs today. According to the report, the big cheeses keep themselves carefully out of the fray; young Albanian men, lured by the promise of quick cash, make deliveries inside Switzerland, which they enter on tourist visas. After a maximum of 90 days, they have disappeared. They know little of the operation for which they work.

So if you're not severely addicted and haven't tried other therapies to kick the habit, you'll end up paying some francs for your stuff after all. The most bang for your buck is to be had in Geneva. A gram of the impure stuff the Albanians are selling (10–15 percent pure, stretched with caffeine and paracetomol) is enough for five fixes; at 20 francs per gram, that's 4 francs a hit. About the same as a cup of coffee—but a much more powerful high.

---

1   And with cocaine. A 2016 European Monitoring Center for Drugs and Drug Addiction study based entirely on sewage analysis found that Zurich is one of the leading cities for coke use in Europe, coming in third place after London and Antwerp out of 50 European cities.

18

Is Switzerland the Most Mountainous Country in Europe?

- Europe's highest mountain is in Russia. The next two highest are in Georgia.
- The European country with the greatest mountainous area is Norway, followed by Spain and Sweden.
- The European country with the highest average elevation is Georgia, followed by Andorra.
- The Alps are shared by eight countries, with the largest shares held by Austria (28.7%), Italy (27.2%) and France (21.4%).
- Europe's longest glacier is in Norway.
- The highest mountain in the Alps is on the Italian/French border.
- The European country with the largest mountain population is Italy, followed by Spain and France.
- The country with the greatest percentage of its *territory* in mountainous terrain is Andorra.

- The country with the greatest percentage of its *population* in mountainous terrain is Andorra.

It looks like Switzerland is getting creamed. In many people's eyes, it started out as the favorite in this competition. After nine rounds, however, there hasn't been a single Swiss victory. The other contestants are neck and neck, with Andorra and Norway in the lead, and Russia, Italy, Austria and Georgia packed together just behind them.

But what's this? It looks like Switzerland is making a move!

- Of the 82 4,000-meter peaks in the Alps, 48 are in Switzerland. Italy comes in second (35) with France a distant third (26).

And see now! Georgia has been disqualified! The judges are ruling that the border between Europe and Asia is formed by the Caucasus, which places Georgia firmly in Asia. This will make for some hard feelings, since many Georgians think of themselves as Europeans, and want to join the EU. But the judges are sticking by their ruling.

And see again! Andorra has also been disqualified! The judges have learned that Andorra is ruled by two *Co-Princes*, and one of those princes is the president of France. This means Emmanuel Macron is competing with a double entry, which is completely against the rules.

So we need to reconsider the points that Georgia and Andorra won—highest average elevation, greatest percentage of mountain area, and greatest percentage of mountain population. The judges are furiously reviewing the Nordic Center for

Spatial Development's 2004 report entitled *Mountain Areas in Europe*—which also leaves out both Andorra and Georgia, lending authority to our judges' tough decisions.

- For highest average altitude, the new winner is: Switzerland! With an average altitude of 1,350 meters, it handily beats out Austria (910), Macedonia (741) and Spain (660).
- For greatest percent of mountain area, the new winner is: Switzerland! According to the report's criterion for "mountainousness," Switzerland's percentage of mountain area just edges out Norway's, 94% to 93%—with Greece a distant third at 78%.[1]
- For greatest percent of mountain population, the new winner is: Switzerland! With a mountain population of 84%, Switzerland easily beats out Slovenia (65%) and Norway (63%), with Austria (50%) a distant fourth.

THE FINAL RESULT: With the greatest number of 4,000-meter Alpine peaks, the highest average elevation, the greatest percentage of mountain area, and the greatest percentage of mountain population, the winner is:

SWITZERLAND!

---

1   The analysis uses the following fairly liberal definition of "mountainous" (read on at your own risk): For altitudes less than 300 meters, an area is "mountainous" if the standard deviation of the 8 cardinal points surrounding it on a one-kilometer grid is greater than 50 meters. From 300 to 1,000 meters, "mountainous" means that altitudes within a 7 kilometer radius vary by 300 meters or more. From 1,000 to 1.500 meters, if the slope to the 8 cardinal points surrounding it on the grid is 5 degrees or more, a point is considered to be in a mountainous area. From 1,500 to 2,500 meters, this slope only needs to be 2 degrees. Finally, *any* terrain over 2,500 meters is considered mountainous.

What a comeback! What a match! Switzerland now reigns as the most mountainous country in Europe. Join us for the next version of this competition, scheduled for March 5, 10,002,018—at which, given the pace of geological change (see Questions 12, 48 and 53), Switzerland will be the overwhelming favorite to retain the title.

19

What Was Switzerland's Major Export in the High Middle Ages?

In *Hamlet*, Act IV, Scene 5, King Claudius, alarmed by the mob at his gate, cries out "Where are my Switzers? Let them guard the door."

Claudius employed Swiss soldiers as mercenaries—as did kings and princes in France, the Netherlands, Spain, Naples, Bavaria, Sicily, Prussia, Austria and Great Britain. For hundreds of years the Swiss were the most feared fighting force in Europe.

Switzerland's major export in the High Middle Ages was war.

Swiss soldiers began selling their services in the early 13th century. What began as an individual or small group business became a state service—the cantons made good money by hiring out whole companies under Swiss command. And these companies were the best: up until the early 16th century the Swiss method of fighting was unbeatable. A square formation of breast-plated men carrying pikes surrounded an inner core of soldiers wielding halberds. With the pikes lowered and dug into the ground, this Swiss *Schlachthaufen,* or battle pile, resembled a massive hedgehog, and easily broke up enemy attacks; the pikes then drew apart and let out the halberds to slaughter the discomfited foes. Swiss troops were notoriously ruthless. They took no prisoners, and were strongly motivated by the plunder that was part of their pay.

In 1516, just as artillery was beginning to poke holes in Swiss invincibility, Thomas More published his satire *Utopia.* In it he described the Zapolets, a mercenary folk who are, as More pointed out in a marginal note, "much like the Swiss."

[The Utopians] hire soldiers from all places for carrying on their wars; but chiefly from the Zapolets, who live five hundred miles east of Utopia. They are a rude, wild, and fierce nation, who delight in the woods and rocks, among which they were born and bred up. They are hardened both against heat, cold, and labor, and know nothing of the delicacies of life . . . Great numbers of them will frequently go out, and offer themselves for a very low pay, to serve any that will employ them: they know none of the arts of life, but those that lead to the taking it away . . . There are few wars in which they make not a considerable part of the armies of both sides: so it often falls out that they who are related, and were hired in the same country, and so have lived long and familiarly together, forgetting both their relations and former friendship, kill one another upon no other consideration than that of being hired to it for a little money by princes of different interests; and such a regard have they for money

*that they are easily wrought on by the difference of one
penny a day to change sides.*

Although More's satire may exaggerate, the Swiss truly did
sometimes fight on both sides of a battle. In the 1709 Battle of
Malplaquet, for example, 8,000 Swiss mercenaries lost their
lives—some fighting for the Bourbons of France and Spain,
the rest for the coalition of the Habsburgs, the United Provinces, England and Prussia.

When the exported merchandise got old, it returned home, im-
porting cash. The English playwright and editor Joseph Ad-
dison visited Switzerland in 1702 and had a look at the wares.

*The inhabitants of the country are as great curiosities as
the country itself. They generally hire themselves out [as
mercenaries] in their youth, and if they are musket-proof
till about fifty, they bring home the money they have got
and the limbs they have left to pass the rest of their time
among their native mountains. One of the gentlemen of the
place, that is come off with the loss of an eye only, told me
by way of boast that there were now seven wooden legs in
his family, and that for these four generations there had not
been one in his line that carried a whole body with him to
the grave.*

The trade in death began to decline in the 18th century, and
the export of war was gradually eclipsed by exports of cattle
and cheese, textiles and watches. Yet Swiss soldiers were still
being employed in Paris at the time of the French Revolution.
The Lion Monument in Luzern recalls not a patriotic battle,

but rather the 850 soldiers of fortune who were massacred during the storming of the Tuileries Palace in 1792.

In 1848 Swiss "foreign service"—as the mercenary trade was known—was outlawed by the new constitution. Only one exception was made, and Switzers still stand outside the Vatican with halberds in hand. Today the Pope is the only man on earth who can still say, with Claudius, "Where are my Switzers? Let them guard the door."

20

What is the World's Most Valuable Banknote?

The most valuable banknote in circulation that hasn't been discontinued is the Brunei 10,000-dollar note (worth over 7,000 Swiss francs). Sorry. The Swiss 1,000-franc note comes in a distant second.

There are even more valuable banknotes still in circulation, but whose production has been discontinued: the US 10,000-dollar note (of which 336 are rumored to exist), and the Singapore 10,000-dollar note, which, though it may be traded in for a Brunei 10-grand at banks in Brunei and Singapore, still manages to be worth slightly fewer US dollars[1]. If we wanted to include notes that are not in circulation but are still being held as legal tender in banks, we'd have to consider the Bank of England's 1-million and 100-million-pound notes, which turn our Swiss candidate into small change.

---

1   Don't ask me—I have no idea.

We're talking about value here, not denomination, so the Zimbabwean 100-trillion-dollar note wouldn't do us any damage, even if it *were* still circulating.[2]

Notes of high value are being discontinued around the world due to fears that they are mostly used by criminals. In 2016, the European Central Bank stopped printing 500-Euro notes—known in some countries as "Bin Ladens." The UK had already withdrawn them from sale in 2010. At that time Ian Cruxton, the deputy director of the Serious Organised Crime Agency, commented:[3]

> *There's been a significant body of evidence over time that has recognised that high denomination notes are an important means of reducing the bulk of cash. The 500-Euro note is really the note of choice among criminals . . . We estimate that more than 90 percent of the 500-Euro notes that are provided in the UK have actually gone into the hands of serious organised criminals.*[4]

The Swiss National Bank disagrees. A spokesman in 2016 said the bank believed the size of a banknote had no impact

---

2   Even as it was printed, this note could barely buy a loaf of bread. *No* Zimbabwean dollars are in circulation anymore: the country hasn't had its own currency since 2009. At the time of the Zimbabwean currency's demise, one US dollar was worth 2,621,984,228, 675,650,147,435,579,309,984,228 Zimbabwean dollars, which rendered them kind of pointless. This happened after a period of 79.6 *billion* percent inflation.
    Ironically, the note is now a collector's item—and a hot one. Selling on eBay for about 30 US dollars, 100-trillion dollar notes have turned into a phenomenal investment.
3   Otherwise known as SOCA. Yes, there really is such an agency. Its sister organization, the Lighthearted Organized Crime Agency (LOCA) has been rumored not to exist, but I haven't been able to confirm this.
4   The more laid-back organized criminals seem to have preferred smaller notes.

on efforts to combat crime. Rather, "The high proportion of large denominations indicates that banknotes are used not only as a means of payment but also to a considerable degree as a store of value."

Store of value indeed, I can hear SOCA seriously muttering. *But for whom?*

In any event, whoever's got them, there are a hell of a lot of them out there. That "high proportion" is amazingly high: some 60 percent of the 55 billion francs that exist in banknote form consists of 1,000-franc notes.

And 55 billion in banknotes is HIGH. Here Switzerland takes out Brunei and, more surprisingly, crushes both the US and the Euro Zone. If you collected all the Swiss banknotes in circulation in one pile, and all the US banknotes in another, the Swiss pile would be worth twice the US one. Given that the US has forty times Switzerland's population, it's remarkable that it only circulates half as much cash. Somebody's storing some Swiss value, and how.[5]

And it's easy to store. While a million dollars weighs ten kilograms in US bucks, it's just a kilo of those purple Swiss notes, and fits into a Tetra Pak one-liter drink box.[6]

A new issue of the 1000-franc note is planned for 2019.

---

5   Switzerland only comes in second here too, though. A pile of all the paper Japanese Yen would be worth more than the Swiss pile.
6   Just about. The official word is that a million will take up 1.3 liters of space. I'll bet you could squeeze them into that Tetra Pak, but I have to admit that, due to circumstances beyond my control, I haven't yet tried.

21

Who's Got the Safest Grave in Switzerland?

On the night of March 1st, 1978, some two months after Charlie Chaplin's death, body-snatchers invaded the cemetery in the small village of Corsier above Vevey and stole his coffin—with him inside it. They demanded a 600,000 dollar ransom from Chaplin's family. When Chaplin's wife Oona wasn't interested—"Charlie would have thought it rather ridiculous," she said—the ransomers threatened their young children.

Police tapped Oona's phone and placed surveillance on over 200 phone booths in the region. On May 17th, the body-snatchers were themselves snatched from one of those booths; they led police to a cornfield just over a kilometer from the Chaplins' house, where they dug up poor Charlie.

Charlie was buried again in the same location as at first, but this time Oona had a two meter thick slab of concrete laid down. In 1991 she was herself laid down inside it, and it was sealed according to her instructions. Which makes Charlie's grave pretty much impenetrable.[1]

---

1   And Oona's.

*   *   *

Body-snatcher Roman Warda was sentenced to four and a half years in prison, while his accomplice Gantscho Ganaz got an 18-month suspended sentence. These relatively light punishments might reflect a peculiar Swiss attitude toward graves: they're temporary resting places. There's even a word for this: *"Grabruhe"*—grave peace—the period of time one gets to lie peacefully in the ground.

Switzerland doesn't have a lot of room to waste on graveyards, so most Swiss graves today are *rented*. The lease usually runs for a *Grabruhe* of 25 years. After that, out comes the gravestone and any decorations, flowers, and so on; the topsoil is turned over; grass is planted; and the inhabitant gets another 10 to 20 years of rest—only unmarked this time. After that, in goes the next one—giving a new meaning to the euphemism, "sleeping together." Coffins and urns alternate in the individual grave sites, perhaps to maintain some kind of decorum. The gravestones can be returned to the owner, but most owners aren't interested—so, at no cost, they're smashed into gravel and ultimately made into roads.

Swiss graveyard gardeners usually turn over entire rows at a time, "so that the graveyard maintains its fine form even after the clearance," as one local official put it.

Mark Twain observed a slightly different system at work in Zermatt in 1878:

> As I understand it, a family owns a grave, just as it owns a house. A man dies and leaves his house to his son—and at the same time, this dead father succeeds to his own father's grave. He moves out of the house and into the grave, and

his predecessor moves out of the grave and into the cellar of the chapel.

So what did the cellar of the chapel look like?

In that cellar the bones and skulls of several hundred of former citizens were compactly corded up. They made a pile eighteen feet long, seven feet high, and eight feet wide. I was told that in some of the receptacles of this kind in the Swiss villages, the skulls were all marked, and if a man wished to find the skulls of his ancestors for several generations back, he could do it by these marks, preserved in the family records.

The tenacity of the bones in Zermatt may have to do with the soil and climate. Grave diggers in the lowlands report that after 25 years there isn't much left of either a coffin or a skeleton.

In any case, none of this is Charlie and Oona's concern. First of all, because they're dead, and second, because they're encased in two meters of concrete—secure against the expiration of any lease.

22

Was Switzerland Built by the Italians?

Much of Swiss infrastructure—dams, roads, buildings, tunnels, railroads—was in fact built by Italian "guest workers." As the Swiss railroads were being built in the last half of the 19th century, for example, Italians at times made up 80 percent of the work force. While in 1860 there were only 10,000 Italians living in Switzerland, by 1900 employment on Swiss construction projects had brought that number up to 110,000, and in 1910 to 200,000.

The Italians were generally poorly integrated—the Swiss marriage rate with Italians was at the bottom of the list of foreign marriages—and were often resented. In 1893 some 60 unemployed young Swiss men, who blamed the Italians for their own inability to land jobs, rioted in Bern. They attacked Italian construction workers; Italian shops, cafés and restaurants were looted. Three years later similar riots broke out in Zurich.

Working and living conditions were often appalling for the mostly young men who came from Northern Italy looking for jobs in Switzerland. The first Gotthard train tunnel was built almost exclusively by workers from impoverished villages outside of Turin. They did not live well:

> *The corridors are as mucky as wet dirt roads; before the doors lies trash; on many of the windowsills excrement is caked, as on the floors, which also often serve as latrines . . . In a house with 240 inhabitants there was a pile of feces that was being removed with a shovel. Another house, with over 200 workers, has no latrine at all—in other houses bathrooms are present, but nailed shut; in others they stand open, but despite this the corridors look no better, and feces lie all around the outside of the houses beneath many of the windows.*
>
> *From these corridors, doors lead to other doors and tiny rooms, each one its own apartment, with from two to four beds and an iron cooking stove. The floors are not merely black from the unavoidable iron and oil of the workers' boots, but also from unaccountable filth; the walls are hung with clothes and moldy sausages; the windows are smudged, clouded, and carefully locked shut. The so-called beds consist of a pile of boards, seldom a real bed-frame, a sack of poor corn-straw, a sheet or not, 1–2 blankets, and often a pillow— everything smeared and black. There the workers lie, wrapped up, two or three in a single bed, in their clothes, often still wearing their boots, as they came out of the tunnel. It is difficult to describe the filth and the stink—therefore we would like to emphasize, for the sake of clarity, that most of the privately rented rooms in Göschenen can only be compared to badly ventilated henhouses, or stirred up boxes of manure.*

This report was commissioned by—and then ignored by—the Swiss Federal Council in 1876.

* * *

Working conditions in the tunnel were no better than the living conditions outside. Deaths on the job were frequent, and company accountability was nil. A typical death notice issued by the Gotthard Railway Company read: "Worker Bianco Giuseppe from Valsavaranche, Piedmont, was run over by a locomotive and died immediately, due to his own lack of care." Another death, reported by the *Handelskourier* newspaper, demonstrates the cavalier attitudes of the foremen to their workers' safety:

> *On the 6th of July the section engineer informed the company of the dangerous passage. On the 7th the engineers no longer dared to pass the spot. On the day of the accident workers were however ordered to go there under the threat of immediate dismissal from their jobs . . . The police, who wanted to go inspect the area on Saturday, were turned away by the foreman.*

Another newspaper, the *Tagwacht,* pursued the matter further.

> *A true murder. And the police are ordered away from the scene? And not a rooster crows in protest? Most newspapers report this story with the same tone as if a pig-stall had collapsed somewhere. Are we going to abide these murders until the last Italian turns his back, trembling, on our "Land of Freedom?"*

Abiding these murders went down fine, apparently, with the Swiss Federal Council. Federal Councilor Hammer wrote to Federal Councilor Welti as follows:

> *Enclosed please find for your perusal a report from the police commando of Canton Uri along with the dossiers*

concerning four accidents which happened in March during the work on the Gotthard tunnel. It seems that all four accidents happened due to bad luck or a lack of proper attention on the part of the victims, and there seems to be no cause for further measures. Thus we consider it obvious that there is no need for us to check on the police administration in Uri.

On July 27, 1875, workers were ordered into the smoky innards of the tunnel to an area where they were unable to breathe because the ventilation system had been shut down to save energy for drilling. They protested but were ordered to stay and work, at which point they walked out and were joined by their colleagues in a strike. A thousand workers faced off with a quickly assembled force of 25 police and deputies, mostly amateurs, on the 28th. The workers threw stones. The police shot bullets. Four workers died. The next day Canton Uri presented the construction company with a bill for 2,510.75 Swiss francs, for services rendered in the incident.

The Swiss Federal Council, pressured by the Italian government, organized an investigation—by one of its cronies. As the investigation began, the Federal Council president let it be known that "It would be most deeply wished, if it would be attested that revolvers were shot by the workers before they were fired by the side of the police team."

Strangely enough, the report came to exactly this conclusion, despite the fact that all eyewitness reports, and even the initial accounts of the police, flatly contradicted it.

Some 2,600 workers were employed to dig the tunnel at any one time. The youngest worker was twelve years old. Workers were paid 3.80 per day (at a time when a kilo of bread cost almost half a franc), two-thirds of which was deducted for food and lodging. Payment was in part by coupons which were only redeemable at the company store. Workers had to cough up an additional 5.- for their lanterns and .30 per day for lantern oil, 5.- per month for clothing and, as a coup de grace, 2.- per month for permission to reside in Switzerland. Three percent of their pay went to the company's internal health insurance, which was used to recompense the severely injured. The loss of a leg was worth 1,650 francs, a hand 1,350, and blindness (generally a consequence of faulty explosives) went for 5,000.

The *Oberingenieur* (chief engineer), meanwhile, was earning 40,000 francs per year in addition to lucrative bonuses.

The First World War and the poorly performing Swiss economy in its wake stopped the flow of immigration, and the Italian population in Switzerland was down to 96,000 in 1941. But after World War II a second wave of Italian workers streamed in: as many as 100,000 arrived in both 1947 and 1948. From the mid-50s the majority of them were from southern Italy. Many of them were seasonal workers with 9-month visas. Not only was integration not promoted—it was actively discouraged. The Italians were thought of as a buffer—a store of workers to be let out and in as unemployment rose and fell— and integration might have got in the way of this flexibility.

The 1960s saw a change in anti-integration policies, as Swiss industry began to depend on workers who would stick around. Naturalization requirements were loosened, work permits were issued after five years of seasonal work, and conditions and insurance were made equal to those for Swiss workers. This led, however, to strong reactions. The Anti-Italian Party was founded, and a popular initiative (see Question 7) that would have booted 350,000 foreigners out of Switzerland at one go was proposed by the right-wing populist James Schwarzenbach, who considered the "brown sons of the South" as "the outgrowth of another species." Restaurants hung up signs reading "Forbidden to Dogs and Italians," and the initiative came close to passing, chalking up 46 percent of the vote in an exceptionally high turnout.

The oil crisis of 1973 braked the Swiss economy and led to high unemployment. Over 300,000 foreign workers left Switzerland, largely exporting the problem. Partially due to this, and partially, perhaps, to the influx of immigrants from countries less familiar to the Swiss, the negative climate for Italians has eased. A 2017 referendum on loosening citizenship requirements for third-generation residents passed with 60 percent of the vote. Of the 25,000 affected residents, the great majority are Italians.

The first Gotthard train tunnel was built almost exclusively by Italian workers. The new Gotthard Base Tunnel (see Questions 3 and 51) had a workforce that was only 22 percent Italian—still the highest percentage of any of the 15 countries represented. Living conditions, in metal containers piled atop one another, were hardly luxurious, but far more sanitary this time around; work was noisy, hot, around-the-clock, exhausting and dangerous, and three of the nine fatal accidents happened to Italians—but worker safety was a high priority for the construction companies this time, and the death rate was low, as tunnels go.

So yes, Swiss infrastructure was in large measure built by Italians. And the numbers from the new tunnel suggest that it is still being built by them—but neither to so great an extent, nor in nearly as appalling conditions, as a couple of Gotthards ago.

23

Is Cannabis Legal in Switzerland?

In the summer of 2016 the owner of a smoke-shop made an unusual trip. He brought a sample of marijuana *to* the police and asked for the go-ahead to sell it in his shop. The police confiscated the weed and told the man to go home.

The marijuana was sent to a lab to be tested. Several weeks later, the police gave the man his grass back. With permission to sell. The stuff had a THC content of less than 1 percent. As such, like various products already on the market—such as a cannabis ice tea in Selecta vending machines nationwide—it was a legal product.

This visit to the police station set off something of a revolution. Since July of 2017 you can buy cannabis cigarettes in Coop—one of Switzerland's two major supermarket chains. The brandname of these ciggies is *Heimat* (Homeland). Meanwhile, in the discount supermarket Denner you can buy a tin of Black Widow pot blossoms to roll yourself. (Not so *Heimat*, since the weed is grown in Vienna.) A company called Valora, which owns the K-Kiosk, Press & Books, and Avec shops, also began selling Black Widow in October in thousands of shops, mostly in train stations.

Powerful marijuana has a THC content of about 20 percent, so the stuff on sale in these mainstream shops is not exactly heady. A component of cannabis called CBD will see to the main effect, which is to reduce anxieties. Yet the cannabis available in the '60s had a THC content of only between 2 and 5 percent. It doesn't take a brilliant mathematician to calculate that two or three joints of Black Widow will give you the same high as one rolled with the grass of the hippies.

The 20 percent stuff still sounds more interesting, though. And so, as I write, are the laws. Article 19b, Section 1 of the Swiss drug law reads as follows:

> *A person who prepares a small quantity of a drug for his or her own consumption, or for the communal and simultaneous consumption of another person of more than 18 years of age, is not liable to punishment.*

And what's a "small quantity?" Funny you should ask. Article 19b, Section 2 continues: "Ten grams of a drug with effects like cannabis counts as a small quantity."

This is all very fine—only in Article 19a we read that "A person who intentionally consumes an illegal drug will be punished with a fine."

So you're allowed to *prepare for consumption* up to 10 grams of weed. You just aren't allowed to *consume* it. This is a fine point of law, which, if transferred to other areas, would lead to such principles as that you are allowed to *prepare* a terrorist attack (as long as it's a small one)—you just aren't allowed to actually set off the bomb.

But things get even better. Article 19, Section 1, Paragraph b states that "A person who illegally possesses, keeps, buys, or in any other way acquires drugs" will be punished with up to three years in jail or a fine.

So you're allowed to *prepare* your weed for consumption but you're not allowed to *consume* it or even to *possess* it.

Something had to happen here. And it did. On a January evening in 2015 two young men in Zurich were stopped by the police, who searched them and found a small bag of marijuana in one of their pockets. The pot weighed eight grams. The young man was made to pay a fine of 100 francs plus 150 francs in fees.

This young man had a friend named Till Eigenheer who was a law student and took on the case. Up until Till offered his free services, the police had tokers in checkmate—the cost of hiring an attorney to argue a 100-franc fine would be ridiculously out of proportion to the possible benefit—so people just paid the money and got on with it. Till, however, advocated from passion. He argued that having a bag of marijuana in your pocket was equivalent to *preparing* to use the drug, and thus could not be punished. As quoted in the weekly newspaper *Schweiz am Wochenende,* Till later said, "The judge smiled at me when I entered the courtroom. And after the trial he congratulated me."

Needless to say, Till won the case. The judge categorized the eight grams of weed in the baggie as a small quantity prepared for personal consumption, and Till's friend was spared 250 francs. But the police were not impressed, and continued to levy fines for possession of marijuana.

Until September, 2017, when the Supreme Court agreed with Till. *Duh!* said the court. Possession of less than 10 grams is "obviously" not punishable. At this point the police in Cantons

Zurich and Geneva, among others, gave in and halted the practice of fining people for possessing small quantities of weed.

It's not over yet, though. First of all, because while the police won't levy fines, they still confiscate the goods. Till Eigenheer argues that if it's not punishable to carry the weed, it can't be legal to confiscate it. As I write, this issue is still up in the air.

There are not a few interested parties to this debate. A 2015 study in *PLOS one,* reviewing data from the Health Behavior in School-Aged Children surveys from 2001 to 2010, found that 39 percent of Swiss 15-year-old boys had smoked cannabis—the highest percentage in any of the 38 western countries investigated. When we add the girls to the mix, Switzerland comes in a close second to Canada. The Swiss Federal Office of Police, meanwhile, estimates that from 25 to 35 tons of cannabis may be consumed in Switzerland every year—but adds that the actual figure may be double that. If that's the case it would translate into 9 grams of pot per year for every man, woman and child in the country. Just under the legal limit for . . . preparing.

Remember *Heimat?* It turns out, according to the same police statistic, that most Swiss buy Swiss: 75 percent of the weed consumed in Switzerland is domestically grown. That *Made in Switzerland* branding campaign seems to have worked on the black market as effectively as it has in the shops.

24

Why Can't I Have a Pet Rat in Switzerland?

For the same reason that you can't have a pet guinea pig.

You *are* allowed to have *two* pet rats (or guinea pigs), however. The reason for this is that rats and guinea pigs are social animals, and get lonely by themselves. Furthermore, according to the regulations of the Federal Office for Food Security and Veterinary Affairs,

> *Rats are extraordinarily playful, love moving about, and are curious. Therefore a rat's home must be large enough and equipped with many opportunities for playing, hiding, and entertainment.*

In case you were now thinking of getting *two* rats (or guinea pigs), it's not recommended. Here's the official bit about guinea pigs:[1]

---

1   There's a very similar bit about rats.

Guinea pigs are very social animals and are not allowed to be kept singly. Their entire liveliness only becomes evident when they are humanely kept in a group of at least two, but better three or more . . . An ideal group of guinea pigs consists of two or more females and a castrated male. In purely female groups there are often quarrels.

So really you need three guinea pigs (or rats). But it's not over yet. Let's say you were trying to do your best and actually bought two rats. You've just learned that to be really humane you need three. What to do? You might think the thing to do is go buy another rat. But no:

The introduction of new members to a group is not very easy. Rats recognize one another by smell, and new arrivals are fought against. Experts suggest that whenever you bring new rats into a group, you bring them in in pairs.

Okay, so now you've got four rats. But not really, because you actually don't have any rats at all yet—you're just thinking about it. And I know what you're thinking now. You're thinking that your daughter, who loves little furry creatures, will surely provide enough company for a single rat (or guinea pig). Think again.

"Human beings can in no way substitute for members of the same species. Guinea pigs can only be lively and happy in a group of other guinea pigs."

Foiled again. But now you're probably thinking that the pet rabbit you already own will be plenty of company for your guinea pig. After all, they're both small furry animals.

Rabbits and guinea pigs cannot satisfy each others' social needs for members of the same species. They can be kept together but only if the pen is large enough and generously outfitted. In this case, however, there should be at least two or three members of each species.

No end run there. Just face it: if you want rats, or guinea pigs (or rabbits now), you're just going to have to invest.

And the whole thing gets much more complicated, because these critters sometimes die. What if you have two rats, and one kicks the bucket? You now only have one rat, which means you're a criminal. You go to the pet shop to get back on the right side of the law, and the owner won't sell you one rat, because rats are social animals. You don't want to confess to your crime, so you buy two rats. But you can't do that either, because those two rats know each other and will pick on the one rat you already have. (Remember, when introducing new rats, you have to do so in pairs.)

Basically, you're screwed. You really should have kept three rats, as suggested. Then when one dies, you can introduce two more to the remaining two. Of course you'll now have four rats. You only ever wanted one.

You can never get out of this!! Once you have rats, if you decide you don't want rats anymore, you have nowhere to go. You can't wait for them to die off, because that would inevitably mean that you reach a point with one rat left—which is illegal. And you can't get rid of them any other way. Why? Because everyone else in Switzerland is fully aware of all the regulations and *no one* is going to take your rats off your hands because that would put them in exactly the same cursed state that you're in now. Your only hope is that your last two rats will be unhappy in love and commit a double suicide.

This rarely happens.

In order to test whether the Swiss actually obey these laws, I tried to buy a rat myself, undercover, in two different pet shops. I was immediately informed, in both of them, that I would have to buy at least two rats. The saleswomen explained carefully that they were forbidden by animal protection laws to sell me just one, and, despite my best efforts, they were not to be talked into fudging this point of law.

So I'll just have to be content with no rats. Which is actually fine by me. I never wanted a rat in the first place.

25

Does Swiss Cheese Cost More Than It Used To?

In the year 1777 the English priest William Coxe, who worked as a tutor for noble families, accompanied one of his charges on a trip through Switzerland. Coxe was a stickler for details. He wrote up his observations in his book *Travels to Switzerland,* and included an account of the making and selling of Gruyère cheese. In this account he notes that "The cheeses fit for exportation weigh from forty to sixty pounds each, and are sold from 1£ 17s to 2£ per hundred-weight." He also describes the means of transport and storage:

> *The casks for exportation contain ten cheeses, excepting those destined for Italy, which hold only three, in order to be conveyed by mules across the Great St. Bernard. The cheeses well packed up bear the transport into the most distant countries; they ought to be kept in a damp place, and frequently washed with white wine, to preserve them from insects.*

Coxe's numbers allow us to do some calculations. The average annual inflation rate of the British pound from 1777 to 2017 was 2.12 percent, meaning that the £2 paid by Coxe is equivalent to £309 of today's money. A "hundred-weight" is approximately 51 kilograms, so £2 (1777) per hundred-weight translates into about £6.06 per kilogram in 2017.

Today you can buy Gruyère cheese at Sainsburys in London for £13.50 per kilo, so just over double—in real terms—what it cost 240 years ago.

Nevertheless, when Coxe says the cheeses are sold for £2 per hundred-weight, he's probably referring to how much the farmer sold the cheese to the exporter for, not how much the cheese cost in London. So let's see what happens if we try to buy it directly from the farm in Switzerland. That will surely be less expensive, and maybe closer to what Coxe would have paid.

Many farms have little refrigerators set up outside with money boxes on them, and you can buy your cheese on the honor system direct from the producer. No middleman, minimal infrastructure, no storage or transport costs. This ought to be a very good deal.

Hmm. No middleman, minimal infrastructure, no storage or transport costs—and 20 francs per kilo, or about £15.30. I'd do better to go to Sainsburys.

Let's go to another farm, one that runs a real shop for direct sales of Gruyère—not just a public refrigerator. This may be more legit.

This time it's 22 francs per kilogram!

The moral of the story seems to be, go buy your Gruyère in London.

To get more scientific about the matter I asked *Switzerland Cheese Marketing* and *Interprofession du Gruyère* what an exporter pays for Gruyère today. After quite a bit of hemming and hawing, they gave me a reasonably straight answer: 12 francs per kilo—or about £9. This is—in real terms—about 1.5 times as much as Coxe would have paid in 1777.

The real value of Gruyère in British pounds, then, has increased very, very slightly, by an annual average of 0.17 percent over the last 240 years. It may not have been a killer investment, but it has kept its head above inflation. The only problem might have been the insects and the mold—but with liberal doses of white wine and a suitably damp place, Coxe's great-great-great-great-great-great-great-great grandchildren[1] might be thanking their lucky stars for their forebear's financial foresight.[2]

Our question, however, is a misleading one in at least one sense: the *meaning*, if not the value, of money was very different to a Swiss farmer in 1777 than it is today. At that time Swiss peasants lived in what is known as a "natural economy," which means they didn't use money much at all. John Murray described the situation in 1861 as follows:

An Englishman, accustomed to buy everything, can hardly realise the domestic economy of a Swiss peasant. He has patches of wheat, of potatoes, of barley, of hemp, of flax, and, if possible, of vines; his own cows, his own goats, his own sheep. On the produce of his own land and flocks he feeds; his clothes are of homespun, from the wool of his sheep; his linen and the dresses of the women of his family are made from his own flax or hemp, frequently woven by the women . . . The timber he requires for his house or for firing is supplied from the land of commune or parish, either

---

1   Coxe married late and had no children, but you get the idea.
2   On the other hand, if you factor in the cost of all that wine . . .

for nothing or a very small sum. What little money he requires is derived from the sale of cheese.

Marie Métrailler, a farmer and weaver from Evolène, depicted this natural economy from the inside:

Grandmother described how, in her youth—and in mine too, for that matter—the farmers only bought two things outside of our valley: salt and iron . . . With our own goods we were never hungry, even if we possessed little. Everyone lived from their own cheese, grain, the potatoes that found their way into the valley at the end of the last century, a bit of vegetables and the meat of an animal which one had raised for a year and slaughtered in the autumn. That's it. In the village we had handworkers of all kinds: weavers, spinners, fullers, sattlers, shoemakers, carpenters. When we needed something, we usually paid in kind [i.e., with other goods or services]. Our basic needs were covered. We lived a life of complete self-sufficiency, a closed economy. And we felt a lot more free. No one demanded anything from others, no one owed anyone any money.

Not only did money form an almost insignificant part of the peasant economy in 1777, the money itself was a different animal than it is today. The Swiss Franc was only introduced in 1848, before which time a whole range of monies were printed and stamped by the cantons and the banks.[3,4] Over 36 Swiss currencies existed, not to mention dozens of foreign ones that were simultaneously in circulation.

---

3   When francs were introduced in 1848, they were all coins. The first Swiss franc banknotes were printed in 1911. In London. At Sainsburys.
4   Just kidding. About Sainsburys, that is. The first Swiss banknotes really were printed in London, though, in 1911.

So when we ask whether cheese was more or less expensive, while the answer is fairly straightforward for a well-off British consumer, we should realize that for a Swiss producer we're comparing apples and oranges. It's not just that the Swiss franc isn't what it used to be—it's that it didn't used to be at all. Nor did the smorgasbord of monies that preceded it comprise the dominant element in economic life—something difficult for most of us to conceive of today.[5]

---

5   For a lovely description of this smorgasbord here is the English writer Fynes Moryson in 1617: "Now I add that the money of Schaffhausen and Constance is spent to the confines of Schaffhausen, and the money of Basel is spent from thence to Basel. At Zurich six Pfenning make a Shilling, and three Pfenning make a Sicherling. Two great Sinsers of Basel, and one little Sinserlin, make a Batz of Basel, and in like sort five Sinserlin make a Batz, and five Sinsers make two Batzen, and these moneys are spent to Strassbourg. Bern, Fribourg and Solothurn have a peculiar money, whereof two and forty pounds Troy weight (in Latin Assis) and twice four ounces (in Latin Trientes) make a gold Gulden. Besides they coin a piece of money, which the Switzers call Dickenpfenning, and the French call Testoone, but it is less worth by the tenth part than the Testoone of France. At Bern sixteen Batzen are esteemed for a Rhenish gold Gulden. The money of Luzern is like to that of Basel, but only six ounces Troy weight more base, and fifty of these moneys make a Rhenish gold Gulden. As the French gold is spent with gain in Switzerland, so in all places upon these confines of France the French silver coins called Francs are commonly spent. In the cantons dwelling scattered in villages a Pound is a Dollar. In Graubünden the bishop and the citizens of Chur coin money . . . and here sixty Creitzers make a common Gulden, four Angster make a Creitzer, and twelve Angster make a Behmisch. But in this province [Graubünden] . . . the Lires or Berlingots, and the Gagets of Venice are vulgarly spent, and I remember that when I came out of the state of Venice into this province, I spent Crowns of Italy; and I find in my notes, that at Lasagna I changed a silver Crown for eight and twenty Batzen; but since seven Batzen of Germany make two Lires of Venice, and a gold Crown of Italy is there given for eight Lires, I think that either it was a gold Crown that I changed, or that the Batzen of this province are of less value than those of Germany. For a gold Crown of Italy, and the French Crown are both of a value, and I said before, that at Strassbourg I changed each of these Crowns for four and twenty Batzen: yet to the contrary I find, that passing forward in the territory of Graubünden, I exchanged at Lanzi a silver Crown of Italy for seven and twenty Batzen, and that three Batzen were there esteemed at fourteen Creitzers, which in Germany are only worth twelve Creitzers . . ."

26

Could the Whole World Sleep in Switzerland?

Switzerland is a beautiful, wealthy, happy country. Notoriously, things work there. Great social services. When you think about it, why shouldn't everybody want to come live here? And I mean, e*verybody*.

Apparently the right-wing Swiss People's Party (SVP) started thinking about this a few years ago, and actually started to get extremely worried about it. It seems they felt that *everybody* just wasn't welcome. So they got together a popular initiative (see Question 7) against *Mass* Immigration. They were accused of harboring xenophobic, sometimes racist, almost fascist tendencies—in part because their campaign posters seemed to deliberately echo a Nazi propaganda aesthetic. They were accused of trying to sabotage Switzerland's relations with the rest of Europe, since the initiative was incompatible with bilateral agreements with the EU on the free movement of persons. But I think they were just confused. I think they overrated Switzerland's attractiveness, and were seriously worried that *literally everybody in the world* might want to move to their small country. And they honestly thought there just *wasn't going to be enough room.*[1]

If so, they were wrong. There are 7.6 billion people in the world, and 41,285,000,000 square meters in Switzerland. If *everybody* moved to Switzerland, each earthling would get an area of about 5.4 square meters. This translates into a square 2.33 meters on each side—slightly larger than a king-sized bed.

In Manila, the most densely populated city in the world, each person gets 24 square meters—a square almost 5 meters per side, in which you could fit *four* king-sized beds, plus some extra space for keeping your shoes. So Switzerland would be about five times as crowded as Manila. Yet the Philippines is a pretty happy place—the *Gallup Global Emotions Report* (see Question 54) ranks its people as the fourth-happiest in the world. So this might not be so bad after all.

We could say that everybody should bring their own king-size bed with them—which would be kind of like their home. The beds would have extremely adjustable legs, because most people like to sleep on level surfaces, and if there's one thing Switzerland is not, it's level. But with adjustable legs, everyone would have a nice horizontal surface to lie on, even if their particular square happened to be on a cliff—which is why I said *extremely* adjustable. Some of these legs might end up being hundreds of meters long.

From high above, the country would look like a kind of massive checkerboard. And it would give yet *another* new meaning to the phrase, "sleeping together." (See Question 21). We would *all* be sleeping together.

---

1   The initiative was approved by the sovereign, earning 50.3 percent of the vote.

Some of us, admittedly, would be sleeping in lakes and rivers, with long, strong bed legs fixed to rocks at the bottom of the waters. Others would be sleeping on glaciers, under lots of duvets. Many others, as already implied, would peer over the edges of their beds and see a *long* way down. We could put all the world's hermits on such beds.

Traveling around Switzerland takes on a new dimension when you think of it like this. Just imagine beds, everywhere you look. The vineyards, the cities, the pastures, the alps: all beds. One gigantic slumber party for the *entire world*.

It sounds kind of nice. I think the SVP should think again. And if they accuse me of leaving out a few practical matters, like food and drink and work—well, I think I could probably accuse them of leaving out a few practical matters too.

Like the fact that, when you invite lots and lots of people to a slumber party, they usually don't *all* come.

27

Do Swiss Cows Commit Suicide?

On August 23rd, 2009, 28 cows landed at the bottom of a cliff near the alp Sous above Lauterbrunnen. Eerie photographs taken from the top of the cliff show a pile of bovine corpses, an image so disturbing that it is difficult to place. Eight years later, during the night of May 24th, 2017, 13 cows sprang off a cliff near the village of Levron in Valais.

The cows above Lauterbrunnen had to climb 200 meters up to a pass and then descend a couloir to reach the cliff from which they plunged. The herd, consisting of 30 mothers and calves, was not regularly milked, and the corpses were only found a couple of days after the fall. Two of the herd had turned away from the rest before reaching the cliff, and were found in good health. The grass above the cliff had not been grazed, indicating that this was not a case of dangerous bovine gluttony.

The cows near Levron broke through several enclosures to reach their cliff. On their way they passed through a pasture on which four yaks were grazing. The yaks were unharmed. Of the thirteen cows who ran off the cliff, one, who landed on top of the others, survived and was helicoptered to an animal hospital in Bern.

Cows rarely fall off of cliffs. When they do so, excepting in these two instances, it is clearly a case of unintentional slipping on steep ground, and happens singly.

In neither case was any evidence found of a predator that might have chased the cows. Neither the dead cows, nor the surviving two above Lauterbrunnen, nor the yaks near Levron had any tooth or claw wounds—nor were there prints or fur or any other traces indicating an attack. Cow experts agree, in any case, that cows disperse when chased by a predator, and that it would be highly unusual for them to flee in a compact group.

Neither of these incidents has been explained.

The most widely held ideas about animal suicide are attached to lemmings. A 1958 Walt Disney "documentary," part of the *True Life Adventure* series, contained a segment in which great numbers of lemmings hurled themselves off of a cliff. The narrator intoned:

> *A kind of compulsion seizes each tiny rodent and, carried along by an unreasoning hysteria, each falls into step for a march that will take them to a strange destiny . . . They've become victims of an obsession—a one-track thought: Move on! Move on!*

The lemmings approach a precipice above the ocean and . . . "This is the last chance to turn back—yet over they go, casting themselves out bodily into space!"

This Disney "documentary," however, was a hoax. A 1983 investigation by the Canadian Broadcasting Corporation found that it had been filmed in Alberta, a landlocked province that is not home to lemmings. The lemmings had been bought from Inuit children in Manitoba, two provinces away. Their compulsive "moving on" was filmed on a snow-covered turntable. And they didn't jump off a cliff: they were *thrown* off the precipice by Disney cameramen. Lemming suicide, says wildlife biologist Thomas McDonough, "is a complete urban legend."[1]

So much for lemmings. More relevant to real animal suicide is a 1999 BBC report about an elderly female elephant named Damini. Damini's younger friend had died in childbirth.

> *She shed tears over her friend's body . . . Over the next 24 days she barely nibbled her diet of sugar cane, bananas and grass, until her legs swelled up and she collapsed. She then lay still, losing weight and crying, and a week ago stopped drinking her daily 40 gallons of water, despite the hot weather.*

Although she was given intravenous infusions of glucose and vitamins, Damini never got up again.

Stories of animal suicides go way back. In 1845 the *Illustrated London News* reported on a "handsome black Newfoundland" who was seen to "throw himself in the water and endeavor to sink by preserving perfect stillness of the legs and feet." The dog was rescued repeatedly, but as soon as he was set free, he went back into the water and tried again. Finally, "by dint of keeping his head determinedly under water for a few minutes,

---

1   For an exposé, see the September 2003 edition of *Alaska Fish and Wildlife News.*

he succeeded at last in obtaining his object, for when taken out this time he was indeed dead."

The former dolphin trainer Richard O'Barry speaks of Kathy, one of the stars of the 1960s television show *Flipper,* looking him in the eye, sinking to the bottom of a tank and purposely ceasing to breathe.

Two millennia earlier, Aristotle reported on a stallion who jumped off a cliff after realizing he had been duped into mating with his mother. The Romans believed that the suicide of horses was a common occurrence.[2]

Hans Heinrich Sambraus was professor of Animal Behavior at the University of Munich at the time of the mass cow death above Lauterbrunnen. He was considered the cow expert above all experts, and was nicknamed the *"Rindermann"*—the Cow-man. His explanation:

> *The occasion for the stampede above Alp Sous might have been very banal. Maybe a cow started running for some insignificant reason, and the others got caught up in it. Since the slope they were on was steep, possibly these 600kg animals couldn't stop themselves and so fell to their deaths . . . There must have been a number of contributing circumstances that happened to coincide.*

Sambraus doesn't want to hear of animal suicide. And nor do most other animal experts. Animals may react to stresses with unnatural self-destructive behavior, they say, but they do

---

2   There are hundreds of other examples of animals killing themselves. Thomas Joiner of the University of Florida details many of them in his book *Myths About Suicide.* Pea aphids, for example, can literally explode themselves in the presence of a ladybug, "scattering and protecting their brethren and sometimes even killing the ladybug. They are literally tiny suicide bombers."

not commit suicide. Ajit Varki of the University of California at San Diego argues that "suicide is inducing your own mortality. But how can you induce it if you don't know you have mortality? It's therefore quite logical that suicide should be uniquely human."

Other researchers disagree, however, and see both animal and human suicide as analogous responses to intolerable conditions. According to Edmund Ramsden's 2010 study in the journal *Endeavor,* animal suicide can change our picture of the human variety:

> *It becomes reversed, in a sense . . . You begin to challenge the definition of suicide. The body and mind are so damaged by stress [that] it leads to self-destruction. It's not necessarily even a choice.*

So, do Swiss cows commit suicide? Or do they merely kill themselves? The question has become academic. One thing, at least, we can say for sure: occasionally, en masse, they throw themselves off cliffs.

28

What Does the Rest of the World Think of Switzerland?

In 2015 the Swiss broadcaster SRF asked some of its foreign correspondents—veteran Swiss reporters who lived abroad—what their host countries thought of their homeland. As might be predicted, the further away the correspondents were stationed, the more the standard clichés reigned.

From San Francisco came a positive image dominated by chocolate, watches, mountains, cows, and a perfectly functioning society—with a slightly negative tinge due to banks that accept money from dictators, criminals and tax evaders. In Washington DC, essentially the same perceptions prevailed, but there was an additional (erroneous) association with the royal palace in Stockholm.

In Russia, the correspondent reported that the Swiss "chocolate side" dominated. Russians found it hard to believe that Switzerland had any heavy industry, and that not every Swiss citizen owned a bank. Switzerland, here too, was often confused with Sweden.

In India, Switzerland is known as an exorbitantly expensive paradise regularly featured in Bollywood films. It's a highly desired destination for honeymoons, and a safe haven for corrupt Indian money.

Closer to home, the pictures become less idealized. Switzerland is rarely given much thought in England, but when it does come to mind it brings up negative clichés of greed and lack of solidarity, coexisting with bucolic images from *Heidi*. The French find the Swiss slow and conservative, and associate Switzerland with rising right-wing populism. In Belgium Switzerland is rarely thought of, and when it is, tends to call up vague notions of anti-foreigner popular initiatives (see Questions 7 and 26). Belgians who have actually visited Switzerland talk of high mountains, clear lakes, and punctual trains. In Germany, meanwhile, Switzerland represents economic success, dependability, precision, and political stability—but also a country that is progressively alienating itself from the EU.

In 2013, the *Neue Zürcher Zeitung* (NZZ) reported on perceptions of Switzerland in China and concluded that, in most Chinese minds, Switzerland is simply "replaced" by Sweden. Both are wealthy European countries, their Chinese names (Switzerland: Ruishi; Sweden: Ruidian) are very similar, and, except for those who have visited one or the other of them, they simply meld.

Chocolate, mountains, watches, cheese, banks, greed, punctuality, xenophobia and . . . Sweden, Sweden, Sweden. The same NZZ article describes the typical, wearyingly familiar dialogue between Swiss tourists and natives of Asia or America: "I'm from Switzerland." "Aha, from Sweden." Not even Switzerland's closest neighbor is immune: the German newspaper

Bild, reporting in 2018 on the World Economic Forum in Davos, included a photograph of a "Swedish special forces soldier" keeping watch from the roof of a hotel. The editor's comment, on being made aware of the mistake, summed up the international difficulties: *"Schweiz. Schweden. Schwierig."* (Switzerland. Sweden. Difficult.)

Sometimes it works the other way around. On April 3rd, 2018, the Swedish music streamer Spotify's direct listing on the New York Stock Exchange was celebrated by the hoisting of a Swiss flag outside the exchange's home at 11 Wall Street. The NYSE changed flags when the mix-up was noticed, and tweeted, "We hope everyone enjoyed our momentary ode to our neutral role in the process of price discovery this morning"—thereby pointing out another confusing factor: the neutrality embraced by both of the Sw . . . countries.

What to do? A satirical piece in the Swiss online news service *Watson* describes a survey in which US high school students place Stockholm and Göteborg in Switzerland. This prompts the US Department of Education to rename Switzerland "Sweden II" in future maps and textbooks. This will reduce embarrassing faux-pas, and is a less expensive measure than adding more geography lessons. With the money saved, American teachers will be outfitted with handguns.

On a more serious note, in 2013 the Swedish and Swiss consulates in Shanghai launched a joint campaign to encourage people to distinguish between their countries—complete with a competition for the best creative work serving that purpose. With 200 entries out of a population of 24 million, the campaign may not have had a decisive impact. Nevertheless, a Mrs. Chen won a 12-day trip to both countries for her short film: "A five-minute intensive course on the differences between Sweden and Switzerland."

Maybe the US Department of Education should get its hands on that film.

29

Is Switzerland Bad for the Environment?

Not as bad as Sweden.

But still pretty bad. The Global Footprint Network calculates that it would take 3.1 Earths to regenerate the resources consumed if everyone on the planet were living like the Swiss.[1] The Federal Office of Statistics goes them 0.2 worse in a brutal confession:

> *[The Swiss] lifestyle is not sustainable, because Switzerland consumes 3.3 times the amount of natural resources that are available per capita worldwide. We are therefore living at the expense of future generations and of other regions of the world.*

The Swiss have been living on credit, as it were, since before 1961—the first year for which the GFN provides figures. Back in '61 they were already using up 1.28 Earths.

---

1   The latest data are from 2013.

Switzerland is hardly the worst offender. In 2005 the US was consuming on the assumption that we had six planets at our disposal; it was down to five by 2013. This is good news in relative terms, but awful in reality. Sweden also does significantly worse than Switzerland, using up four Earth's worth of resources. The Swiss could get offended and make this point the next time someone thinks they're from Sweden, but somehow saying, "Hey, I only use up three planets—they use four," doesn't seem a very satisfying retort.

The world leaders in terms of sustainability are clustered in the Indian subcontinent and sub-Saharan Africa, where resources are still consumed at a better than sustainable rate. Eritrea, the world leader in sustainability, consumes only 0.3 Earths. But that comes at the cost of nearly universal poverty.

Three-fourths of Switzerland's ecological footprint is due to the consumption of fossil fuels. This is true despite the facts that Switzerland's electrical power comes almost exclusively from hydro and nuclear plants, that it has the most intensively used railway system in the world, and that its recycling practices are among the world's best: 52 percent of industrial and household refuse was recycled in 2016.[2]

The 2016 *Global Wealth Report* by the Credit Suisse Research Institute tells us that the average Swiss adult is the wealthiest of any country in the world—by far. She holds assets worth 560,000 dollars, leaving her closest competitors in the US (345,000) and the UK (289,000) in the dust. Not to mention the average earthling, whose holdings, at 53,000 bucks, are worth less than a tenth as much.

---

2   The Swiss railway system runs 90 percent on hydroelectricity, and by 2025 aims to get 100 percent of its energy from renewable sources.

When we turn to the environmental footprint, however, we see the Swiss consuming resources at a 3-planet pace, while the average over the whole globe is 1.68. Shall we commend the Swiss for having over *ten times the wealth* but using *less than twice* the resources that the average inhabitant of planet Earth does? Shall we compare her to the average American, who, with only 60 percent of the Swiss person's wealth, manages to consume 170 percent as many Earths—i.e., three times as many planets per dollar? In both comparisons, the Swiss seem to come off well—likely due in large measure to their trains, their dams, their byzantine recycling system, and a certain native frugality and lack of ostentation.

Switzerland may indeed come off well in such comparisons. On the other hand, 3.1 Earths is—well, 3.1 times as many as we've got.

30

How Much Would It Cost to Buy Switzerland?

Actually, you can't buy the whole thing. Much of it is owned by the state and won't be sold. But I can arrange for you to buy all the rest.

So let's go. First we're going to buy up the forests, which account for almost a third of Swiss territory. Wooded land is not often for sale, but it's relatively inexpensive when it is: 2 to 3 francs per square meter. The thing is, only about 30 percent of Swiss forest is privately owned—the rest belongs to towns, cantons, and the federal government. Still, you could buy a fair amount of wooded land—close to 4,000 square kilometers. It'll cost you 11 billion francs.

About a quarter of Swiss land—some 10,000 square kilometers—is agricultural, and goes for 6 to 10 francs per square meter. This tab comes to 80 billion francs.

Then comes the expensive stuff: the settlements and urban areas. These make up only 7.5 percent of Swiss territory, but get very pricey. Land in Zurich will cost you over 3,000 francs per square meter. The cheapest you can get anywhere will run you 200. Using a ballpark figure of 2,000, you'll get your 3,000 square kilometers for about 6 trillion francs.

The rest, I'm sorry, you can't have. The alpine pasturelands, whose area makes up 12.4 percent of the country, belong to the towns or the alpine cooperatives, and won't be sold. And the remainder—the high mountains, the cliffs, glaciers and scree, the lakes and rivers, and the wetlands and scrub—which together make up a quarter of Switzerland—belong to the cantons.

You've agreed to purchase 40 percent of Switzerland, though—about 16,000 square kilometers—and it'll cost you some 6,091,000,000,000 francs.

Now it's time to play hardball. We're going to buy all the buildings.

According to a 2014 study for the Federal Office of Housing, Switzerland contains some 2.5 million buildings, over two-thirds of which are residential. The 2013 market value of all these buildings was around 2,739,000,000,000 francs—that's almost 3 trillion. This translates into approximately four times the Swiss Gross Domestic Product—or, if you like, four times the US defense budget. On the other hand, all this real estate is only worth about half of the assets managed by Swiss banks.

We're not buying what's *in* the buildings, mind you. No furniture, no gold, no art, no oil, no enriched uranium. We'll let people take that with them. We're just buying the buildings and the land.

I have to give you some disappointing news, however. Most people don't want to sell. They're perfectly happy with their houses and their yards, their fields and their forests. So we're going to have to tempt them with an offer they can't refuse. I can act as your agent, but you're going to have to send me a LOT of muscle. Especially since you're buying EVERY-THING, so everyone's either going to have to rent from you or move out of the country.

Oh, and I'm going to be wanting this in cash.

So let's look at that cash and see how many suitcases you need to fill with it. As we learned in Question 20, a million francs in those sleek purple 1,000-franc notes takes up a volume of about 1.3 liters. You now owe me about 6 trillion for the land and almost 3 trillion for the buildings, so lets call it 9 trillion francs. A little multiplication shows you owe me 12 million *liters* of tightly packed purple notes.

I assume you'll be bringing the dough in from outside, and flying it into Zurich, so let's examine the planes you'll use. A cargo-carrying 747-400F jumbo jet has a maximum capacity of about 750,000 liters. That means you're going to have to send 16 jumbo jets packed full of bills. If they're crammed into extra-large cabin suitcases of 50 liters each, that makes 240,000 suitcases. Each stuffed to the gills with 1,000-franc notes.

I'll be waiting for you with a few 40-ton trucks that I'll use to carry the cash around Switzerland. Well, more than a few. About 135 of them. Traffic might have to be re-routed for a while. But hey, nobody's going to complain about blocked traffic. We've made them an offer they can't refuse.

I've just thought of another problem, however. And it makes this whole project suddenly look unrealistic. It's this.

We need 9 trillion francs, in 1,000-franc notes. They don't exist.

If you study Question 20 and do some arithmetic, you'll find there are only 33 billion francs worth of purples in the entire world. We need over 270 *times* as many of these bills as are in circulation.

I think this pretty much squashes our plan. Maybe you should go buy some other country. Switzerland's too expensive.

31

How Late Are Swiss Trains Every Day?

Swiss passenger trains arrived "on time" at 88.8 percent of their stops in 2016. "On time" is defined by the Swiss Federal Railways (SBB) as "not more than three minutes late"—which may sound like a strange definition of "on-time," but is less strange than the German Federal Railways' (DB) definition, which is "less than five minutes late." If the Swiss applied the German definition, their trains would be 96.8 percent on time. It's a neat little trick the Germans are playing there.

Nevertheless, since Swiss trains log in almost 20 billion passenger-kilometers every year, those "less than five minutes" add up, as do the 3.2 percent of Swiss arrivals that are more than five minutes late. Passenger-kilometers are just what they sound like: the number of kilometers each single passenger travels added all together. If one person rides a train for 10 kilometers, that's 10 passenger-kilometers, but if two people were on the same train, it would be 20 passenger-kilometers.

If a single person were to travel all of the person-kilometers that Swiss trains lay down in a year, she'd be able to travel to the sun and back more than 65 times.

* * *

Similarly, if a train is 10 minutes late to arrive at a station and one person gets off there, we have a lateness of 10 person-minutes. But if two people get off at that station, there is a total lateness of 20 person-minutes, even if the train was only 10 minutes late.

The SBB published an interesting statistic in 2014: the number of person-minutes their trains were late over the course of the entire year.[1] That number turned out to be 141 million. This makes for an average of about 386,000 person-minutes per day.

To picture how late that is, we can imagine that all the trains on a given day are exactly on time—except for one. Luckily, on that one train there's only one passenger—a woman commuting to her office, which is right near train station X. Everybody else gets to their stations right on the money, and this one passenger is the only one who's late. So when would she show up for work?

Since we're talking 386,000 person-minutes, but there's only one person involved, that person has to be 386,000 minutes late. 386,000 minutes is 286 days. Our passenger arrives at work a little over 9 months after she was expected.

She'll probably get fired for her gross lack of punctuality. In fact, by now they've probably forgotten all about her.

On the other hand, she has a pretty good excuse. Her train was late.

---

1   They have since stopped publishing this statistic.

32

Were the Swiss Alps Conquered by the British?

If you look up "The Golden Age of Alpinism" on Wikipedia you'll come upon the following sentences:

> *The Golden Age of Alpinism was the decade in mountaineering between [British] Alfred Wills's ascent of the Wetterhorn in 1854 and [British] Edward Whymper's ascent of the Matterhorn in 1865 . . . The golden age was dominated by British alpinists and their Swiss and French guides. Prominent figures of the period include [list of eleven British]. Well known guides of the era include [list of nine guides].*

In *Killing Dragons: The Conquest of the Alps,* Fergus Fleming concurs:

> *Exploration conjures up images of obsessive men—typically British—doing mad things in strange surroundings. The Alpine explorers were no different. Always fixated and sometimes peculiar, they shared a background of illness and phobia: sickly childhoods were ubiquitous; insomnia and*

indigestion were common; one man was afraid of heights, another of garlic. They had spiritual problems, being uncertain whether the Alps would lead them to God or confirm his non-existence. And yes, a lot of them were British. Then again, a lot of them were not.

While both Wikipedia and Fleming make a nod to the non-Brits, it is always the British who are mentioned first, who "dominate," who are "prominent." The guides follow, mentioned almost as an afterthought.

A more accurate picture is presented by a magnificent bronze sculpture in the Casino Square in Meiringen. Two men, well known in mountaineering circles, are climbing up a mountain ridge (not of bronze—it's a real boulder). The one in front carries a coil of rope in his right hand, an alpenstock in the left, and seems to be leaning into a rough wind; the one behind, tied into the other end of the rope, looks comically startled, his left hand reaching toward his head—for his hat has just blown off, and lies a good meter away from him on the rock.

The man in front is the Meiringen native Melchior Anderegg, known as the "king of the mountain guides"; the one behind is a Cambridge University fellow, journalist, editor, president of the Alpine Club, and father of Virginia Woolf.[1] He is Leslie Stephen, one of the foremost of the Golden Age generation of British climbers.

The "conquering of the Alps" almost always proceeded as in the sculpture in Meiringen—namely, with a Swiss guide in the lead. Leslie Stephen confirms as much:

---

1   The Alpine Club is the British Alpine Club, which, being the first and only alpine club at its founding, did not find it necessary to specify its nationality.

The true way at least to describe all my Alpine ascents is that Michel or Anderegg or Lauener [Swiss guides] succeeded in performing a feat requiring skill, strength, and courage, the difficulty of which was much increased by the difficulty of taking with him his knapsack and his employer.

Stephen then adds a respectful note about the character of his guides:

Amongst the greatest of Alpine pleasures is that of learning to appreciate the capacities and cultivate the good will of a singularly intelligent and worthy class of men. Would that an English agricultural peasant were generally as independent, well-informed, and trustworthy as a Swiss mountaineer!

A more accurate rendering of the Golden Age, then—without the heavily British, "Wills and Whymper," slant—would state that it began with Ulrich Lauener's climbing of the Wetterhorn, with Wills in tow, and ended with the Chamonix guide Michel Croz tying his shirt to an alpenstock atop the Matterhorn. But history is written by those who write it, and, often, those who pay for it, and in this case it was both written and paid for by Wills and Whymper.

The Matterhorn climb ended the Golden Age for two reasons. The first is that almost all significant peaks had then been scaled—there were no more Alps to be conquered. The second is that of the seven men in the party that made it to the top of the Matterhorn, only three returned to Zermatt alive. Alpinism lost its innocence with the three corpses carried back to the Zermatt cemetery after their 1,000-meter fall.

Yes, *three*. For while four men fell to their deaths on their way down the mountain, only three bodies were ever found. A boot, a belt, and a pair of gloves of the fourth lay on the ice next to the other corpses, but not the man himself.

That man was 18-year-old Lord Francis Douglas, and his body is expected to emerge from the ice of the Matterhorn Glacier any day now (see Question 5).

Ironically, Alfred Wills's climb up the Wetterhorn, which kicked off the Golden Age, was a mistake. Wills, who later became an English High Court judge, set off from Grindelwald to make the first ascent of the peak—an ascent that had, in fact, already been made. The Wetterhorn had been summited ten years earlier—by two Swiss guides, Melchior Bannholzer and Johann Jaun, who didn't drag up any British gentlemen at all.[2]

We can rewrite the Golden Age in two ways, then. We could say that it began with a Swiss guide's ascent of the Wetterhorn and ended with a French guide standing on the Matterhorn summit. Or, if we really want to go British, we could say that it began with a judge's mistake and ended with a Lord's disappearance. In either case, it was Swiss—and in a few cases, French or Italian—mountain folk who first climbed the Swiss mountains—with the difficulty, as Stephen says, much increased by their British employers.

---

2   Whymper was an exception—not a gentleman but a wood engraver. He was perhaps the most tenacious and independent of the pioneers—yet even he always climbed with guides.

33

How Many Toblerones Would It Take to Make a Matterhorn?

This is a big project. First we cover the Matterhorn in plaster of paris, let it dry, and remove the plaster mold. We'll need somewhere to store it so we'll put it upside down with its point in Zermatt and its base leaning between the Zinal Rothorn and the Obergabelhorn. Things will be a little shady in the valley for a while, but it's only temporary, and the way the mold is leaning will allow the town to get some morning sun.

Then we'll need to get rid of the actual Matterhorn. We'll saw it through at its base and put it somewhere—where?[1] The Swiss have dug a lot of long holes through their mountains; we could try to break up our Matterhorn and jam it into a bunch of tunnels.

---

1   This is not only easier said than done, but more easily said than conceived. Where is the base? There are many ways to define it and none are objectively correct, but I'm going to cut out essentially a pyramid with a 2 kilometer square bottom and a height of 2000 meters. This approximates what a layman would think of as the "Matterhorn," especially as seen from Zermatt, and 9th grade geometry tells me it has a volume of 2.6 billion cubic meters.

The Swiss Tunnelling Society (yes) calculates the total volume of all Swiss tunnels at about 114 million cubic meters. My last footnote puts the Matterhorn at 2.6 *billion* cubic meters. That's way too much rock for the tunnels. We could only fit about a twentieth of the Matterhorn into them. Well, that won't do.

We'll decide instead to dump the Matterhorn into Lake Geneva. Better than dump it, even—we'll *place* it in Lake Geneva. We can put it opposite Lausanne in the middle of the lake, where it's 310 meters deep—so the top 1700 meters of the Matterhorn will stick out of the water. It makes a very steep island. It will be a wonderful tourist attraction and people can go out in boats and paddle around it. Not too close though, as the lower elevation will cause the permafrost to melt and all sorts of huge boulders will constantly be falling into the water—which will make an amazing show, far outdoing the Jet d'Eau in Geneva for hydrotechnics.

Speaking of Geneva, if we do this, will Geneva vanish? The volume of the bottom 310 meters of the Matterhorn is about a billion cubic meters. Dropping it into the lake would cause an enormous tsunami that would kill over a million people—and yes, Geneva would vanish. We don't want that. So we'll lower it in very gently.

The level of Lake Geneva's waters are regulated by the Seujet dam about a kilometer down the Rhône from the lake.[2] The average flow out of the lake is 270 cubic meters per second—about six Olympic swimming pools per minute—but the dam can and regularly does deal with double that. We can arrange this. We'll take 43 days to lower our mountain into the

---

2   The dam's job is to keep the level of the lake at between 371.7 and 372.3 meters above sea level. In the spring of every leap year the level is dropped to 371.5, for cleaning purposes.

lake, never causing more than double the average outflow—and Geneva, rather than vanishing, will hardly even notice.

Having safely stowed away the real Matterhorn, we now have to make the new one. We'll need to pour chocolate into our mold. We're never going to get our hands on enough Toblerones to fill the thing up, since we'll need about three and a half billion tons of chocolate, which is far more than has ever been produced. But we'll enlist the entire Swiss chocolate industry in the endeavor.

Annual chocolate production in Switzerland is 180,000 tons, which is only about 1/20,000 of what we'll need. But we're patient. We'll just have to save up all the chocolate produced in Switzerland for the next 20,000 years.

This is going to get expensive—the chocolate alone will cost about 30 trillion francs, which is one-fortieth the current value of Switzerland (see Question 30)—and we're going to have to hire riot police to quell the disruptions instigated by all the chocolate addicts who are furious at what we're doing because they won't get any chocolate. Or they'll have to go to Belgium.

We pour chocolate into the mold for 20,000 years, then, and finally we're ready to go. We lift the filled-up mold and turn it upside down, right on the spot where the Matterhorn used to be. We remove the mold. We have a chocolate Matterhorn. It's beautiful. Now what are we going to do?

Remember, chocolate addicts have been starved for 20 millennia. There's going to be a massive crowd rushing to this Matterhorn; there will be stampedes and tramplings; the security forces will be overwhelmed. Millions may die. But there's plenty of chocolate. In fact, there are 20 quadrillion food calories in this mountain, which is enough to provide the entire population of the world with energy for two and a half years. If we decide to be fair and distribute it evenly, farmers all across the planet can take a break while our mountain is devoured.

And now, our great work complete, we sit back and think on its beginnings. Why, we ask, did we do all this? And we recall that the shape of the Toblerone bar, and the image of the Matterhorn depicted on its packaging, inspired us to our feat.

A nearby chocolate connoisseur, sitting on his haunches and licking his sticky fingers, laughs. "Is that really why you did it?" he asks. "But don't you know?"

"Know what?" we reply.

"The Toblerone bar," he says, "was invented in 1908. The Matterhorn was stuck on the wrapper in 1970. A silly sales gimmick. It was never supposed to be the Matterhorn. Theodor Tobler decided on the shape of his creation in Paris, at the circus. He was watching a troupe of tumblers form a human pyramid, and—Eureka!"

How easy it is, on a mistaken assumption, to waste 20,000 years of one's life.

34

Why Are So Many Swiss Sheep Killed By Wolves?

From 1998 to 2016 over 3,000 head of well-guarded live-stock, mostly sheep, were killed by Swiss wolves—often in massacres in which most of the dead were left uneaten. The Swiss federal and cantonal governments compensate farmers for their losses when the livestock are adequately protected—by, for example, electric fences or Maremma guard dogs.

Up until the 16th century wolves lived in every part of Switzerland. Traveling in Graubünden in 1617, the English writer Fynes Moryson reported that "Out of the wood near Lanzi [modern Lantsch or Lenz], in the twilight of the evening, I did hear more than a hundred wolves howling." The English diarist John Evelyn arrived in Brig in 1646 and saw that

> *Almost every door had nailed on the outside and next the street a bear's, wolf's, or fox's head, and divers of them, all three; a savage kind of sight, but, as the Alps are full of the beasts, the people often kill them.*

Already by Moryson's and Evelyn's time, however, the number of wolves had begun to plummet. Human settlement took away their habitat; forests were cut down for pastureland, depleting the supply of deer, elk and ibex that were the wolves' natural prey; and wolves were systematically shot by farmers who feared for their livestock and could, at the same time, pick up a bounty for their efforts. In 1890 the last Swiss wolf for over a century was sighted in the northern Jura.

The ensuing respite in the battle between farmers and wolves ended in 1995, when a lone wolf entered Switzerland from Italy. Italian wolves had themselves been driven to the brink of extinction, but the dwindling population had received state protection and began recovering.

By the end of 2017 about 40 wolves had made their home in Switzerland, including four packs that had formed and successfully reproduced—two in Valais, one in Graubünden, and one in Ticino. Wolves enjoy limited Swiss protection—government permits to dispatch them are issued only if the same wolf is shown to have been responsible for massive livestock losses over a limited period of time.

Still, the battle has picked up again. History repeats itself. Pastoralists fight against wildness. The *Association for a Valais Without Large Predators* lit a bonfire of protest in September, 2017. The president of the association announced that, "We want to send a clear signal here today. Because we want neither lynxes, bears, jackals, nor wolves in our region."[1] As one part-time sheep farmer says, "Valais and Switzerland are so thickly settled. The wolf has no place here, in contrast to Alaska, Canada, or Eastern Russia . . . We're not a nature reserve for the amusement of city folk."

---

1   There is no threat of jackals settling in Switzerland.

A comment on an article in the May 20th, 2015 issue of the newspaper *Schweizer Bauer [Swiss Farmer]* hides nothing: *shoot, shovel, and hush it up,* it advises as the best solution for "these beasts the wolves." Maremma herd dogs are a beautiful idea in theory, many farmers argue, but the practice is different: the dogs have daily conflicts with hikers and mountain-bikers, and are not appreciated by neighbors in town when the summer is over and the sheep have come down from the alp.

Particularly frustrating for sheep farmers is the fact that wolves often kill far more sheep than they eat. This casts them as vicious, spiteful, wasteful and destructive, and brings the ever-latent agriculturalist hatred of wolves out into the open.

Wolves are hardly indiscriminate killers, however. In fact, as Barry Lopez points out in his classic work *Of Wolves and Men,* it is very difficult to predict which animal a wolf will choose to take and which it will ignore. Hungry wolves very often turn away from obvious and easy prey.

Lopez suggests that a "conversation of death" takes place between a wolf and a wild animal in a decisive moment of eye contact. Depending on the result of that conversation—which, as for many indigenous human hunters, has a sacred quality to it—the wolf either takes the prey or not.

When wolves come upon domestic farm stock, the "conversation" is missing. As Lopez says

> *What happens when a wolf wanders into a flock of sheep and kills twenty or thirty of them in apparent compulsion is perhaps not so much slaughter as a failure on the part of the sheep to communicate anything at all—resistance, mutual respect, appropriateness—to the wolf . . . They have had the conversation of death bred out of them.*

Wolves don't know how to deal with such a spiritual vacuum and, as it were, they freak out. They kill the sheep out of all proportion to their need—yet, because the sacred quality of the food is absent, they often hardly touch it.

A more conventional view—one which sees animals rather as machines than as discriminating conscious beings—is that the process of hunting, killing, and eating is a step-by-step one for wolves. The killing stage precedes the eating stage. In the wild, by the time a prey animal is downed, the rest have generally fled to a safe distance—and the eating stage begins. With domestic animals, who may be fenced in, or lack a flight instinct, the killing phase will continue for as long as there are animals to kill. Such "surplus killing" is not a characteristic unique to wolves, but is seen in many other predators as well.

Farmers have always been prone to seeing predators who endanger their stock as vermin. For German cattle ranchers in Namibia, majestic lions were simply vicious pests and, like Swiss wolves, were viciously exterminated.

8.5 million Swiss—the wealthiest people in the world—versus 40 wolves. Here we see distilled the millennia-old conflict between pastoralists and wilderness, between civilization and nature, between a view in which human concerns have precedence over all else and one which considers animals and plants, as Yuval Harari puts it, "equal members of a spiritual round table."

Can the Swiss manage this conflict better the second time than they did the first? Or is it too late to go back, even partially, to a world in which wolves are magnificent creatures with whom we share at least certain bits and pieces of our landscape? We shall see.

35

How Large Would Switzerland Be If It Was Ironed Flat?

Switzerland's "footprint" is the two-dimensional area within its borders—the shape you see when you look in an atlas, when you look on Google Maps *without* the 3-D, or every time you see the front of a Chevrolet car.[1] To measure the area of the footprint, you could cut out a huge piece of cardboard exactly the same 2-D shape and size as Switzerland, and a much smaller piece of cardboard only 1 meter square. Now see how many times the 1-meter-square piece fits onto the big piece. If you do this, you'll find it fits about 41,285,000,000 times.

You actually won't be able to do this for several reasons. You'll never find such a big piece of cardboard, and you won't have the time. Even if you're a Swiss man—boasting the world's longest male life expectancy of 81.3 years—and you spend your entire life laying down the smaller piece of cardboard at a rate of once per second, without pausing to eat, drink

---

1   Louis Chevrolet came from La Chaux-de-Fonds, Switzerland. He chose a stylized version of the Swiss footprint for his company logo.

or sleep, it would take you 16.5 lifetimes to measure the Swiss footprint.

Measuring Switzerland's *actual* surface area, the *3-D* one with mountains and valleys, is in principal just as simple as measuring the footprint. Take your 1-meter-square piece of cardboard and start laying it down all over the real Switzerland. It's going to be leaning this way and leaning that way as you do it, and sometimes it will be completely vertical, and sometimes, on overhangs, it will be upside down, but all you have to do is cover the whole country with it and count up how many times you laid it down.

There's a key difference between measuring the footprint and measuring the 3-D area, however. When you're measuring the footprint, it doesn't matter what size square you use. You'll get the same area if you use a 2-meter square, or a half-meter square—you'll just have to make one-fourth, or four times the number of measurements.[2] With the 3-D area it *does* matter. The smaller the square you use, the more little bumps and holes you'll pick up in the terrain.

Thus while the footprint area of Switzerland is a single number, the 3-D area depends completely on the size of your cardboard square. There's no single number that can describe it.

The Swiss Federal Office of Topography measured the 3-D area of Switzerland with a larger square: 25×25 meters. It didn't take hundreds of workers several generations to do this, because they did it on a computer. The area they came up with was 46,710 square kilometers. This is 13 percent more than

---

2   Four because a 2-meter square has four times the area of a 1-meter square.

the area of the Swiss footprint. On this scale, the mountains added 5,425 square kilometers to the area of Switzerland.

One of the Topography Office workers, a man named André Streilein, went even further, however. He estimated what the 3-D area would be if you actually used 1-meter squares, as we've been imagining. As expected, the calculated area was considerably larger: about 80,000 square kilometers. On the 1-meter scale, Switzerland's area was almost doubled by all its mountains.

So what's the *real* answer? There is no real answer; there are only finer and finer scales, each of which makes Switzerland larger and larger. However, I think André Streilein's answer is the most *human* answer.

Human adults tend to be just under two meters tall, and our pace is something less than a meter. If there's a mouse hole or a molehill in the middle of that meter, we just step over it. But if there's a hole a meter wide, we have to react—walk around it, or jump over it, or climb into and then out of it. A 1-meter hole (or hill) makes a difference to us. Thus a 1-meter square approximates how we experience our environment, by reacting to things that we would actually react to.

How big is Switzerland? It isn't. But on a human scale, it's about twice as big as the atlas will have us believe.

36

Where Can I Find Prehistoric Art in Switzerland?

The oldest known form of human art consists of groups of small hollows carved into large rocks. These hollows are known as cupules. Robert G. Badnarik, one of the world's foremost cupule experts, describes them in the following passage:

> *The roughly hemispherical features that we are concerned with here, pounded into horizontal, inclined and vertical rock surfaces, probably constitute the most common motif type in world rock art. They occur not only in every continent other than Antarctica; it appears they have been produced by many of the rock art traditions, transcending all major divisions of human history.*

The Val d'Hérens in Valais has several wonderful cupule stones. Near the Alp Cotter, at a spot with one of the best views in the area, are a whole series of them. The largest is about 2 meters long and 1.5 wide; it has dozens of cupules in it, of various sizes—from 2 to 20 centimeters in diameter. Some of them are joined by channels, some are surrounded by circles, and a few crosses run between the hollows. Other nearby stones have smaller numbers of simpler cupules in them. Sometimes people place bunches of wildflowers in the larger hollows, which collect water when it rains. There are two different cupule rocks in Evolène, 500 meters below Cotter. Zermatt has several fine examples, as does the Val d'Anniviers. Overall, there are over 1,000 cupule sites in Switzerland—most of them rarely visited.

It isn't easy to make a cupule with stone age equipment. Experimenters found it took them 8,490 blows with a rock hammer to create a tiny one less than 2 millimeters deep. A larger one, just half a centimeter deep, took 21,730 blows over two days and left the experimenters suffering from fatigue and pain. These things weren't made by accident.

The earliest known cupules are in Tanzania and date back to 1.74 million years ago. 1.74 million years is about nine times as long as modern homo sapiens has existed, meaning these things were made by lots of hominoids before us.[1] Examples in India date back perhaps as far. Cupules are found on the *underside* of the slab covering a 40,000-year-old Neanderthal tomb in La Ferassie, France. Yet they are also found on church door-frames in Europe dating up to the year 1,000.

Why the hunter-gatherers pounded cupules in the stones of Cotter is obscure. Perhaps, like aborigines in the Northern Territory of Australia, they believed the dust created by the hammering represented the life essence of the rock, and would increase the fertility of nearby animals. Or perhaps, like Pomo

---

1   Homo Habilus, Homo Erectus, and so on.

women in California, they made a paste of the pounded dust and applied it to their skin or their vaginas, impregnating themselves with the rock's magical powers. Perhaps, like the Plamath people in southern Oregon, they hammered to summon changes in the weather—or, like the Hupa, they used them as a kind of calendar. Perhaps, like women in Punjab along the Ganges, they poured sacred water into the hollows in order to increase their own fertility. Or perhaps they placed the umbilical stumps of their babies in the cupules to guarantee their long life, as did indigenous people in Hawaii. Other peoples have used cupule stones as musical instruments, or to communicate with ancestors, or to call assemblies.

Whether any of these varied uses represent the intentions of the people who originally made the cupules is unknown.

Thus we have lots of possibilities, but in the end absolutely no idea what the hunter-gatherers in Alp Cotter were doing with their cupules. We can't even know *when* they were doing it: if the cupules were renewed from time to time with a new round of hammering, scientific dating would only lead us to their most recent renewal. Their origins are lost.

But the cupules are not lost. The oldest and most mysterious hominoid art form sits, unguarded and often unremarked, on stones all over the Swiss Alps.

37

Is Switzerland a Haven for Nasty Dictators?

Ferdinand Marcos (Philippines). Hosni Mubarak (Egypt). Baby Doc Duvalier (Haiti). Sase Seko Mobutu (Democratic Republic of the Congo). Muammar Gaddafi (Libya). Viktor Yanukovych (Ukraine). Sani Abacha (Nigeria). Moussa Traoré (Mali). Bashar al-Assad (Syria). These are but some of the dictators who have stashed their money in Swiss banks.

In 2016 the Swiss Federal Department of External Affairs published a pamphlet entitled "Dirty Money." The article "Switzerland Does Not Want Corrupt Money" opens with this salvo:

> *"I am just a middle man," says Swiss banker Lachaise moments before being killed by a knife thrown to the back of the neck. "I am doing the honorable thing and returning the money to its rightful owner."*
>
> *James Bond of Her Majesty's Secret Service replies sarcastically, "And we know how difficult that can be for the Swiss."*

The pamphlet argues that the Swiss are actually pretty good at returning money. It claims that over the past 25 years some 2 billion francs in dictators' stolen assets have been returned to their plundered countries—more than from any other financial center. It goes on to quote Theodore Greenberg, former Chief of the Money Laundering Section of the US Department of Justice:

> *The old days are over. No despot, no dictator or other klep-tocrat will easily be able to deposit dirty money. Switzerland as a favorite place for criminal or blood money should be a thing of the past.*

The question is, are the dictators paying any attention to the pamphlet? It's notable that these 2 billion francs were all returned *after* the despot in question had fallen from power. And there are indications that the old days just might not be getting over. As recently as February, 2018, the Petrobras affair—one of the worst corporate corruption scandals in Brazil's history—landed in Switzerland. The Swiss Financial Supervisory Authority reported on February 1st that the Lugano-based PKB bank

> *had not adequately identified contractual partners and had failed to carry out appropriate background checks into high-risk business relationships and transactions. The bank was also found to have failed in its duty to report suspected money laundering to the Swiss authorities.*

The old days don't seem to be quite as "over" as Theodore Greenberg suggests.

*   *   *

In 2016 the Swiss Parliament passed the Foreign Illicit Assets Act, which will ease the freezing, confiscation, and return of looted moneys. Oliver Longchamp of the Swiss NGO *The Berne Declaration* doubts, however, that the passage of the bill will make much difference to new deposits.

> *Unfortunately, the new law being debated by Parliament will not change the situation . . . [It] focuses on funds already identified in Switzerland. It will not prevent the influx of illegal money gained from corruption.*

The Swiss Bankers Association tends to agree, using the euphemism PEP, "Politically Exposed Person," for a corrupt dictator: "The problems arise only from the moment the PEP becomes a *persona non grata* in the eyes of the Swiss government or other international organisations."

In 2012 the Swiss Parliament considered and rejected a bill which would require PEPs to prove that their assets had been legally acquired. It seems that Switzerland is more interested in returning money than in refusing it in the first place.

The African continent's longest serving leader is Teodoro Obiang Nguema Mbasogo of Equatorial Guinea. He seized power in 1979, and, according to the BBC, is "one of Africa's most brutal dictators." *Human Rights Watch* claims that "the dictatorship under President Obiang has used an oil boom to entrench and enrich itself at the expense of the country's people." Obiang has been pursued in French courts for plundering state coffers to buy luxury homes and cars. His son Teodorin has been busy fighting US efforts to seize his assets.

Within a six-month period in 2016, an official jet from Equatorial Guinea landed in Geneva 25 different times. This is all the more remarkable because the jet had been banned from European airspace due to safety concerns.

I know that the Obiangs landed in Geneva 25 times in just half a year because I read it on Twitter. Swiss journalist François Pilet has set up a bot connected to a system that tracks the planes of autocratic regimes when they land in Geneva. Each time a dictator's plane lands, out goes a tweet. Here's an example:

As of the end of 2016, the bot was publishing the arrivals of over 80 aircraft from 21 different countries.

Pilet doesn't claim that every one of these flights arrives in Switzerland with an illegitimate purpose. Still, he says,

> *Switzerland is a safe haven for powerful people from third world countries, for leaders who want to stash away the money they have stolen from their people . . . I like very much the idea that each time a leader of an autocratic regime is landing in Geneva on his private jet, the information is made public instantly . . . We should ask ourselves each time: why exactly are they coming here?*

Why indeed? Perhaps, like Sir Leslie Stephen in 1871, they feel that

The Lake of Geneva is almost a sacred place to the lover of mountain scenery . . . Its lovely grouping of rock and hanging meadow and distant snow and rich lowland and breadth of deep blue water strikes one as a masterpiece in some great gallery of exquisite landscapes.

Maybe this is what goes through the Obiangs' minds as that Dassault 900B lands again and again and again at Geneva's Cointrin airport.

But then again, it's probably not.

38

What Happens When You Accidentally Land an Airplane on a Glacier?

Here is a description, by the pilot, of an accidental glacier landing:

> *Fast-moving dark lines below the plane suddenly became a glacier. This did not immediately register—I just knew that we were very close to whatever it was. Later I discovered that the lines were crevasses. As I reached up and threw the throttles, propellers and mixture forward and pulled back on the yoke, I told my co-pilot, "We're in the mountains!" My co-pilot thought I had vertigo so he held his yoke, which kept me from pitching up. I reached over and forced him off the controls and, almost as quickly, I said: "We're on the ground."*

The year was 1946, and the plane an American military Dakota DC-3. On the morning of November 19th, it had taken off from Munich with a four-man crew and eight high-ranking passengers, including generals' wives and an eleven-year-old daughter. The flight's destination was Marseilles. There were political tensions between Switzerland and the US at the time, and American planes were not allowed to fly into Swiss airspace. The pilots had thus planned a course which would lead them across Germany and then south over France.

Weather was bad and visibility poor to nonexistent. The plane hit the glacier at 280 kilometers per hour and slid some eighty meters to a halt, passing huge crevasses as it plowed into the snow. "Mayday! Mayday! USZ68846 crashed," radioed the pilot. The message was heard in Paris and Marseilles. The American military set in motion a massive aerial search action over the French Alps.

Meanwhile, at the Swiss Air Force base in Meiringen, pilot Viktor Hug noticed that the emergency signals were remarkably clear, and deduced that they must have been coming from nearby. He asked for permission to begin a search—but the permission was denied. The only missing airplane was, after all, in France.

It took until Wednesday evening for a triangulated radio signal to reveal that the missing DC-3 was not in France after all, but somewhere in the area between Airolo, Sion, and the Jungfrau. The American military now sent a special train to Switzerland from Italy, with ambulances, Jeeps, M-29 tracked vehicles (a cross between a tank and a snowmobile) and 150 mountain troops. While they were traveling, an American B-29, with the Dakota pilot's father aboard, flew over the Gauli area and spied, through a break in the clouds, the downed Dakota. And so the US soldiers, with all their vehicles, headed for Meiringen.

* * *

The first American plan was to drive through the Urbach valley and into the Gauli basin with the jeeps and M-29s, which would then proceed onto the glacier and reach the plane. To the Swiss who knew the gorges and steep slopes that defined the terrain, this was a blatantly absurd idea, and they successfully talked the Americans out of it. The next American plan was to drop 70 paratroopers and three nurses onto the glacier. The Swiss, who also knew the glacier's vast extent and huge crevasses, rejected this idea as well. Meanwhile US, French, and British planes were air-dropping support packages for the crash survivors. These landed in crevasses, or miles from their target, or so dangerously near the target that, after a sack of coal had smashed into the plane, the survivors wrote "STOP!" in huge letters in the snow. At this point the Swiss forbid the Allies to fly over the area at all.

While all this negotiating was going on, a Swiss rescue effort was under way. Eighty men led by nine mountain guides had set off at four on Saturday morning to climb up from Rosenlaui toward the scene of the accident. A thirteen-hour slog through deep snow, past avalanche slopes, and over the icefall of the Rosenlaui glacier brought them to the aircraft, lodged in snow and ice at 3,500 meters above sea level. The rescue party had no choice but to spend the night there, in temperatures of 15 degrees below zero.

On Sunday morning the exhausted rescue team was dragging the crash survivors down the Gauli Glacier on sleds when Viktor Hug—the man who had originally noticed the emergency signals in Meiringen—and a colleague showed up, out of the air. In small Piper Storch aircraft fitted out with home-made, improvised skids, they landed—very neatly—near the rescue column and began to fly out the victims. Eight round trips later, the job was done—to the delight of large crowds and reporters from around the world, who had gathered at the Meiringen airfield.

The Dakota adventure—with its good and bad glacier landings—marks the first mountain rescue in history effected from the air.[1] And while planes had previously taken off from snow and landed on snow, this was the first time they had taken off with wheels from land and touched down with skids on a glacier.

In the summer of 2012 three young climbers came upon a propeller sticking out of the ice near the bottom of the Gauli Glacier. Since then other airplane parts have surfaced: part of a wing and a piece of landing gear.

The airplane struck the glacier in 1946 at a speed of 280 kilometers per hour. It has since slowed down. In the 70 years after the accident that bit of wing traveled 3.5 kilometers inside the ice (see Question 5). That translates into 50 meters per year, 4 meters per month, and 13 centimeters per day, or 0.00000517 kilometers per hour. Its speed in the ice was one fifty-millionth of its final speed in the air.

---

1   This, at least, is the commonly accepted date, endorsed by the REGA (Swiss Air Rescue). The Swiss Glacier Pilots Association claims that between 1942 and 1945 the pilots Othmar Bloetzer and André Bidel had already rescued about 45 people with ski-landings in the mountains. The Historical Lexicon of Switzerland, however, claims that Bloetzer (who later became Commander of the Air Force) only became a pilot in 1946. Alas, nothing is certain in human affairs. With such confusion about, we'll stick with the Dakota story—because it's the orthodox one, and because it's so good.

39

Is It Ethically Okay to Buy Swiss Chocolate?

The Swiss human rights watchdog *Public Eye* estimates that 2 million children in Ghana and the Ivory Coast are involved in growing and harvesting the cacao that provides so much pleasure to our palates—often under abusive conditions. Fair trade certifications that require farmers not to put their children to work are not much help if the farmers can't afford to hire adult laborers to replace them. Such certifications, while well intentioned, are often riddled with loopholes. They may be more of a balm for European consciences than a bonanza to African farmers.

Chocolate has had a tarnished history from the moment Spanish conquerors—a.k.a. war criminals—first found the Aztecs drinking a frothy brew in Mexico. The European taste for the drink was directly responsible for a significant increase in slavery in the Americas.[1] *Someone* had to work on the plan-

---

1   Solid chocolate was pretty much inedible until Rudolf Lindt discovered conching in Bern in 1879.

tations that produced that delectable bean. And since it wasn't quite as delectable unless it was sweetened, chocolate is implicated in sugar plantation slavery as well.

Today the chocolate market in Asia is exploding, at the same time as monocultures and over-fertilization are rendering the African plantations less productive. Chocolate will be getting more expensive, and the pressure to expand into yet more untouched forest will increase. If history is any indication, chocolate is simply too delicious for child labor, obscenely underpaid farmers and environmental concerns to get in the way of its expansion.

The problems with chocolate are not distinctly Swiss, but the Swiss are heavily involved. A Swiss company you've probably never heard of, Barry Callebaut, is the world's leading cacao trader and processor, while better known names like Nestlé, Lindt and Mondelez (Toblerone) produce a significant portion of the end products. All four of these companies receive a rating of "negligent" from *Public Eye*.

With the average Ivory Coast cacao worker earning 50 cents a day, don't we have to wonder: according to what twisted rationale should these men, women, and children work for wages at one-fourth the poverty level so that Barry Callebaut can make its millions? What do these African farmers owe European chocolate addicts? What do they owe the swanky customers in Asian dessert bars, who eagerly await the latest treats that Callebaut invents in its "Chocolate Academies" in Mumbai, Shanghai, Tokyo and Singapore?

Chocolate tastes so good that it almost feels unethical to ask whether it's ethical to buy it. Most Swiss, in any case, don't seem to: according to Chocosuisse, Swiss consumed

11 kilograms of chocolate per head in 2016—more than any other nation except Germany. That's 110 standard-sized chocolate bars for every man, woman and child in the country. It's also a lot of cacao—and a lot of African children wielding machetes instead of going to school.

40

What Happens If I Commit a Violent Crime in Switzerland?

In March, 2015, a 20-year-old man known to the public as Stephan L. followed instructions on the Internet for making a silencer. He attached the silencer to his father's pistol, stood behind his father as he watched television, leveled the gun at the back of his head, and blew his brains out.

In 2016 Stephan L. was sentenced to five years in prison for manslaughter.

In cases where the law prescribes a fixed range of sentences, Swiss judges tend very much to exercise leniency. Murderers can be sentenced to between 10 and 25 years, but the average murderer who left prison in 2016 had only served 12. Rapists can be punished with between 1 and 10 years, but the average rapist left prison having served 2.5.

Even more astonishing: in 2016 one-third of convicted rapists left the courtroom as free men, with suspended sentences hanging over their heads.

* * *

In 2008 a car sped out of a driveway and slammed into a 67-year old motorcyclist, who died four days later in a St. Gallen hospital. The driver was fined 1000 francs. He was given a suspended sentence of 90 daily 40-franc payments, but he only had to pay if he repeated the offense.

This may all seem mad, but there is a method to it. Swiss justice aims not at revenge but at maintaining the societal integration of the offender and at preventing repeat offenses. Prison terms, arguably, are counterproductive on both counts—as well as being inordinately expensive for the state. Therefore the 2005 revision of the Swiss penal code emphasized the use of monetary punishments and community service in place of jail-time and, in either case, suspended sentences for first-offenders.

The logic goes like this: a suspended sentence—say, two years jail time, or a 2,000 franc penalty—hangs over the head of the offender. He doesn't serve the jail time, and he doesn't pay the penalty, unless he breaks the law again. The first-offender thus has a double incentive not to get in trouble a second time. If he does, he'll not only be punished for the second offense, but will have that dangling penalty from the first one thrown at him as well. Since monetary punishments have been shown to deter crime as effectively as jail time, and since they bring money to the state rather than loading it with the costs of incarceration, the most effective punishment for a crime would seem to be a suspended monetary sentence along with community service. The offender has a double incentive to stay clean, remains integrated in society rather than shut out, and costs the taxpayer a pittance compared to a prisoner.

The judge's job, of course, becomes very subtle. She has to distinguish between those offenders who are likely to repeat anyway, and from whom society needs protection, and those who will take to heart their misdeeds and the danger it has placed them in. Such subtleties are not likely to be delved into in outraged tabloid accounts such as the one cited above involving Stephan L.

Judges will sometimes get it wrong. Fabrice B. was convicted of rape in 1999. He received a suspended sentence of 18 months. In 2013, a social worker was driving him, alone, to horseback-riding therapy. Fabrice B. stopped the car, tied her to a tree, raped her and slit her throat.

The tabloids had a field day. Fabrice B. obliged them by saying that he found his first sentence very mild, "almost a free pass to keep doing it."

By far the greatest number of sentences hung on convicted criminals in Switzerland are suspended. The criminologist Martin Killias points out that

> *There is no country in Europe where people condemned for severe crimes like robbery, child molesting, grievous bodily harm, or rape so seldom go to prison as Switzerland.*

If you want one of these suspended sentences, however, it very much helps to be Swiss. Over 70 percent of the adult prison population in Switzerland is not. According to a study by a team from Bern University, this is not because foreigners commit more crimes, but rather because they are considered a flight risk.

Switzerland's prison population is currently around 7,000, meaning that 83 out of every 100,000 residents is in jail. This rate is slightly higher than Norway's (75) and Germany's (77), less than half that of England and Wales (175), and about one-seventh the rate in the USA (600). This sounds pretty good on the face of it.

Turning the numbers around, however, the picture is bleak. The US justice system is generally condemned as racist because, while African-Americans make up 13.3 percent of the population, they constitute 34 percent of prison inmates. Foreigners in Switzerland make up 25 percent of the population and 72 percent of the inmates. Thus while there are 2.55 times as many African-Americans in prison as there would be in a fair society, in Switzerland there are 2.88 times as many foreigners in jail as there ought to be.

The answer, then? If you commit a violent crime in Switzerland, and it's not too egregious, as violent crimes go, and you're Swiss, and it's your first offense, you'll very likely get a suspended sentence and walk free. If it's egregious—such as rape—you still have a pretty good chance of getting a suspended sentence and walking free, but it's more likely you'll spend some time in jail. If you're a foreigner, meanwhile, you've got a much higher probability of landing in the slammer—or, as they say in German slang, the *Knast*—a word which, ironically, comes from the Yiddish for "financial penalty."

41

Is Swiss Hydropower Really Clean?

I'm going to sell you some electricity. Here's how. I have a big nuclear power plant and a big coal-fired plant. I use the electricity they produce to pump water uphill from one reservoir to another. Then I let the water run back down to the lower reservoir, turning a turbine as it flows, and thereby producing electricity.

As you can see, my electricity is made from falling water: clean hydropower.

Would you like some?

I know what you're going to say. You're going to say it's not clean, because while the *electricity* I'm selling comes from water turning a turbine, the *energy* comes from dirty sources: the coal plant polluting the air and dumping CO_2 into the atmosphere, and the nuclear plant leaving behind radioactive waste that we don't know what to do with (see Question 57).

You'll also probably say that if you intended to buy dirty energy, you'd rather just buy it directly from the coal and nuclear plants. You point out that energy gets *lost* in transporting the water to the upper reservoir and then letting it run back down, so that my electricity is actually even *dirtier* than the stuff you could have bought from the other plants in the first place.

You might even advise me to trash my entire setup, both because it delivers dirtier electricity than coal and nuclear *and* because it's a net consumer of energy rather than a producer— it eats up more electricity than it delivers.

Finally, you might advise me that there's no money to be made by my system, and the sooner I get out the better. And you might even be right.

But if you claimed that no one with any expertise would ever invest in such a system, you'd be wrong. The Swiss energy giant Axpo recently spent 2.1 billion francs building one of these facilities in Linthal in Canton Glarus.

The Swiss Energy Foundation (SES) objects to this system— called pumped-storage, for the same reasons that you objected to the energy I tried to sell you a few paragraphs ago: it "massively increases the consumption of energy"—energy that's dirty in the first place.

So what's the catch? Why did Axpo spend 10 years and 2.1 gigafrancs on their facility? Even Axpo is wondering. Jörg Huwyler, its director of hydro-energy, commented in 2016 that "Under current conditions we would not have built it." Gianni Biasutti, the former director of the hydro giant KWO in Canton Bern, remarked in 2013 that the business model of such systems "has become practically dysfunctional."

There was a time in the recent past, however, when the system was indeed functional. It all had to do with timing. Nuclear and coal plants are difficult to regulate, so they produce energy at the same rate day and night. Industry is quiet and people sleep during the night, so the demand for electricity goes down—and the price of a kilowatt-hour plummets. The trick of pumped-storage plants was to buy cheap nuclear and coal at night, and sell expensive hydropower during the day.[1] What has put a hole in the business plan is not the dirtiness or the waste of the system, but the falling price of electricity—there's no longer enough differential between night and day to pay off all that pumping.

Most Swiss hydropower comes not from pumped-storage systems, but either from seasonal storage or run-of-the-river plants. The latter use the flow of rivers to turn their turbines. Seasonal storage systems, meanwhile, collect water naturally in high-altitude reservoirs, then let the water rush down penstocks (huge pipes) to turn turbines in the valleys. They are seasonal because the reservoirs fill up with summer meltwater, but get depleted in the winter when there's little melt to flow. Such systems produce far more energy than they use, and their energy is largely clean—though they severely disrupt the ecological systems that they alter to achieve their ends.

Yet even some of the seasonal storage plants don't function without pumping. The Grande Dixence in Valais, for example, claims to produce 2,000 gigawatt-hours of clean energy per year. Yet it also *consumes* 400 gigawatt-hours in pumping *up* some 60 percent of the water that fills its huge reservoir. The energy captured from this pumped water is not all clean, for the same reason that the pumped-storage plants' energy

---

1   Hydropower can be turned on and off at will. The Grand Dixence in Valais, for example, can go from zero to a full-on nuclear plant's worth of electricity in under four minutes.

isn't clean—it's bought on the open market, largely from dirty sources.[2]

Some say that the days of pumped-storage plants are over, as coal and nuclear energy are phased out for environmental reasons. But every year almost 1,600 gigawatt-hours of Swiss energy still come from such systems, and many experts argue that pumped-storage will be more necessary than ever in the future. They claim that renewable energy from sources like solar and wind will need to be stored during sunny and windy times and supplemented on calm and cloudy days—and pumped-storage is an optimal way to do this.

The director of the foundation *Landschaftsschutz Schweiz* (Landscape Protection Switzerland), Raimund Rodewald, is not happy with this idea. He puts it in a nutshell: "This is a worrying vision: the Swiss Alps as the battery of Europe."

A battle is likely to rage, pitting the battery against the beauty of the Alps. A first step has been taken: Switzerland's Energy Strategy 2050 has been passed by Parliament and blessed by the Swiss sovereign (see Question 7). The Strategy blurs and weakens once-clearly defined provisions for the preservation of "Landscapes and Natural Monuments of National Interest." Such natural treasures no longer enjoy absolute protection; instead, conservation and energetic interests are to be weighed against each other on a case-by-case basis.

Hydropower in the future may be clean. It may be more. And it may be ugly.

---

2   It's still preferable to the pumped-storage water, however, because it's pumped up fewer meters than it travels down—and thus is a net producer of energy, despite catching a ride uphill.

42

How Dangerous Are Swiss Poisonous Snakes?

In June, 2013, the German reptile expert Dieter Zorn was in Faugères, France, putting on the show he had performed for decades all over Europe. The purpose of the show, according to Zorn, was to help people get over their fear of snakes. While displaying an asp viper—one of the two venomous snakes native to Switzerland—Zorn was bitten several times in succession. He had the presence of mind to put the asp back into its vivarium and shut the lid. He then dropped dead.

The audience's fear of snakes was, arguably, little reduced by the performance.

Both of the Swiss poisonous snakes—the asp viper and the common adder—are very shy, have not the slightest interest in harming a human being, and will do so only if they feel cornered and threatened. Both are protected species that have been largely driven out of their habitats by human settlement, and are now found predominantly in the mountains.

According to biologist Othmar Stemmler in his *Reptilien der Schwiez (Reptiles of Switzerland)*, there is a 4 percent chance of death following the untreated bite of an asp viper, and even less for the common adder.

Old-time farmers who summer their cows, goats and pigs on alps in the Ticino, where asp vipers are common, tell stories of the snakes. They say that vipers love milk, and if you want to draw a viper from its den you should put out a saucer of milk at night and then get up early in the morning and wait for your prey. The love of milk, they say, drives vipers to strike at farm animals' udders, killing goats and inducing miscarriages in pregnant cows. Keeping a turkey is said to be the best way to keep your alp clear of vipers, as turkeys actively hunt them. Another way to rid an area of snakes is to catch one and burn it alive—its hisses of agony are said to scare off all the other vipers in the area.

Wildlife biologists dispute all of these contentions.

No one has been killed by a native venomous snake in Switzerland for over 55 years. The average population of Switzerland over these years has been about 7 million. Even if someone were killed by a snake tomorrow, that would still put the odds of a randomly selected Swiss resident dying from the bite of a Swiss snake in any given year at about 1:400 million.

Meanwhile a randomly selected human resident of planet Earth has a 1:320 million chance of being killed by a champagne cork, a 1:50 million chance of being killed by a falling coconut, and a 1:2.5 million chance of being killed by a hippo.[1]

This makes Swiss vipers seem pretty tame. But be careful when you pop the cork on that champagne.

---

1   Notice that I said a "randomly selected" person. The chance that *you* will be envenomed, clonked by a coconut, crushed by a hippo or brained by a cork depends on how and where you spend your time. If you live the whole year round in Switzerland, you're not likely to meet either a coconut tree or a hippo, though your chance of taking a hit from a champagne bottle is probably relatively high.
     Notice also that I didn't succumb to the temptation to throw vending machine deaths in here. The statistics on vending machine deaths are *very* outdated and unreliable. For a full discussion, see Karl Smallwood's 2017 article in *Today I Found Out:* "Do Vending Machines Really Kill More People Than Sharks?"

43

What Does My Country Have to Do to Buy Arms from Switzerland?

"It has to not be at war, not use the weapons to commit human rights violations, and not re-export the weapons." This, at least, was the answer the Federal Council gave in 2009 when it was arguing against a ban on Swiss arms exports.

Today, however, things are a little different. Because in 2014, having won the argument by defeating a popular initiative (see Question 7), the Federal Council decided that the bit about human rights wasn't such a big deal after all—and so, together with the Parliament, they nixed it.

So a more up-to-date answer is: It has to not be at war, can use the weapons to commit human rights violations or not, as it pleases, and cannot re-export the weapons.

Actually, now that I think about it, Switzerland sells weapons to both the USA and Saudi Arabia. They *are* at war and have been for some time—in Afghanistan and Yemen, respectively. So I guess that first requirement must be some kind of a joke or something, and if we want to give an honest answer, we'd best get rid of it.

So: Your country can be at war (or not, as it pleases), it can violate human rights (or not, as it pleases), but it *cannot* re-export the weapons.

Actually, now that I think about it a little more, Swiss hand grenades have been used in the Syrian civil war, though they were never sold to Syria. Swiss Pilatus planes have been bought by the US, refitted, and then sold to Afghanistan. And Swiss tanks sold to the Saudis have been used to repress demonstrations in Bahrain.

So I guess your country *can* re-export the weapons after all. I think it might work like this: you have to *say* you won't re-export the arms. And then you go ahead and sell them on, just as the US did to Afghanistan.

The final answer, then, appears to look like this: Your country can be at war (or not, as it pleases); it can use the arms to commit human rights violations (or not, as it pleases); and it has to say it won't re-export the weapons.

Maybe the best answer is simply: Your country has to pay hard cash. How about that? And lots: Switzerland is one of the world's top per capita arms exporters.[1] (It's also the largest producer of small arms ammunition in Europe.) Swiss tanks were used by Pinochet to crush the opposition in Chile. Swiss Pilatus planes were used by Saddam Hussein to drop poison gas on the Kurds, by Chad to drop cluster bombs on fleeing refugees, by the Mexican Army to bombard villages in Chiapas, and by regimes in Myanmar, Guatemala, Iran and Angola to bomb their own peoples. I think

---

1   Fifth place, for example, in 2013.

the answer to our question, really, is just that you have to pay hard cash.

This may sound pretty compromised, especially for a "neutral, peace-loving" country. It recalls a comment about Switzerland delivered by the French statesman François René de Chateaubriand two hundred and some years ago: "Neutral in the grand revolutions of the states which surround them, they enrich themselves by the misfortunes of others and found a bank on human calamities."

Now surely that's pretty harsh. But at least the Swiss military-industrial complex hasn't done *really* awful things, like illegally ship arms to apartheid South Africa, help it develop nuclear weapons, and cooperate with its intelligence services. Right?

As it happens, these are some of the questions that the Federal Council asked the Swiss National Science Foundation to clear up in an assignment given in May, 2000. The foundation went at it with a team of historians and researchers—on the condition that they be given liberal access to the federal archives. The Federal Council agreed.

Then, in 2003, the Federal Council suddenly stopped agreeing. They blocked access to the archives, creating, according to the project leader, a "serious disturbance" to the research. Swiss historians had to dig into South African archives to turn up information about Swiss activities to complete an assignment given them by a Swiss Federal Council that was blocking their access to Swiss archives.

And they did turn up information. Here is a summary of the findings by one of the Science Foundation historians, Peter Hug:

*The relationship between Switzerland and South Africa
was politically, militarily, and in terms of the arms industry most intense during the years when the South African
policy of apartheid was most deeply characterized by severe human rights violations and the open use of violence,
namely in the 1980s. Swiss industry circumvented in grand
style the arms embargo that the UN had imposed on South
Africa. The Swiss administration was well informed about
many illegal and half-legal activities, and put up with them
quietly, actively supported them, or half-heartedly criti-
cized them. The Federal Council was not informed about
most of the irregularities and did not take its supervisory
task at all seriously. This also applies to the cooperation
between the two countries' intelligence services . . . which
smoothed the way for the armaments deals, waged a battle
against opponents of apartheid, and spread political propaganda in favor of the South African regime. Swiss industry was one of the pillars of the secret South African
nuclear weapons program . . . and delivered key compo-
nents for the uranium enrichment that provided the necessary fissile material for the six atom bombs produced by
South Africa.*

Okay, okay, I give up. So Switzerland is the world's fifth
largest per capita arms exporter, exports to countries at war,
countries who disregard human rights and countries who
re-export the weapons, AND it illegally shipped arms to apartheid South Africa, helped it make its A-bombs and collabo-
rated with its intelligence services.

And this answer began with such promise . . .

44

If You Balanced Switzerland on the Tip of a Pin, Where Would the Pin Prick?

Some time ago an employee at the Swiss Federal Office of Topography took a 1:300,000 scale map of Switzerland and glued it onto a big piece of cardboard. He took a pair of scissors and cut along the border, then tried to balance his creation on a pin. The pin balanced the cardboard when it pricked somewhere just to the south of Sachseln in Canton Obwalden.

In 1988 the surveyor Martin Gurtner headed to a computer to make this calculation more precise. He came up with the Swiss coordinates 660158/183641—which means the point is 660,158 meters east and 183,641 meters north of an unassuming concrete cylinder stuck into the ground in a vineyard near Bordeaux, France. This cylinder, about 15 centimeters in diameter, and rising some 20 centimeters out of the earth, marks the origin of the Swiss coordinate system—and can be identified by the peeling Swiss flag painted on it.

That the origin of the Swiss coordinate system should be in this particular spot in Bordeaux is no accident. It allows the Swiss grid to fulfill four conditions: all coordinates are positive; no coordinate has more than 6 digits; there is no overlap between east and north coordinates (so if someone reverses the order, it is obvious); and, finally, the coordinates of a spot approximately halfway along the southwest wall of the Exact Sciences Building of the University of Bern are a clean 600000/200000.

Now that Gurtner had cleared up exactly how many meters east and north the balancing point of the Swiss footprint (see Question 35) is from the little cylinder in Bordeaux, the folks at the Federal Office wanted to present this significant point to the Swiss people as a gift. They would set up a large triangulation pyramid at the exact spot, and it would become a tourist attraction—the geographic center of Switzerland!

There was a problem, though: the geographic center of Switzerland happened to lie on steep wooded ground surrounded by cliffs, a place of blueberry bushes and chamois, but definitely not suited for gatherings of human beings. So . . . they cheated.[1] They set up their triangulation pyramid 500 meters to the southeast of the calculated point, on a flat part of Älggialp, and everyone just *pretended* that this was the geographic center of Switzerland.

The point became well known when, in 2002, the Swiss TV broadcaster SRF began awarding a prize to the "Swiss Person of the Year." They presented the award at Älggialp, where the name of the illustrious person was inscribed on a metal plaque attached to a large stone just under the triangulation pyramid.

---

1   Gurtner's words were, *Mer händ es bitzeli bschisse.* Which means, "We cheated a little bit."

SRF ran out of money for this extravaganza in 2015; the last Swiss Person of the Year was Polo Hofer—who, just by the by, was Kim Jong-un's favorite pop star when he went to school in Bern (see Question 15).

The most exciting event in the life of the triangulation point marking a spot 500 meters from the geographical center of Switzerland and sheltering the name of Kim Jong-un's favorite Swiss pop star, however, was its kidnapping. In May, 2009, the pyramid disappeared. No one noticed for a few days because, as a tourist attraction, the pyramid was pretty much a dud—but when a shadowy secessionist group with terrorist leanings tipped off a press agency, the alp warden of Älggialp went up to have a look. The pyramid was indeed missing. A flag of Canton Jura was planted in its stead. A few days later the secessionists, who are fighting to have three towns in Canton Bern transferred to Canton Jura, set up the missing pyramid *at the geographical center of Canton Jura.* The action was a bold one, and shows how potent a symbol the geographical center of a country can be.

Such a potent symbol of national identity ought, however, to get it right. And there are two obvious senses in which it's just all wrong. First of all, if the geographical center of Switzerland is at 660158/183641, it seems profoundly disturbing that the triangulation pyramid is not at 660158/183641, but 500 meters away. This would seem to militate against everything that the Federal Office of Topography stands for, with its beautiful and incredibly accurate maps and the wealth of precise data that produces and extends them. Sloppy work.

But there's an even larger problem. When Herr Knöpfli—for such was his name—cut out his piece of cardboard and balanced it on a pin, he didn't put any mountains on it. His

Switzerland was flat. And if anyone ought to know that Switzerland isn't flat, it's an employee of the Federal Office of Topography. It's perfectly clear that if he had put the mountains on his piece of cardboard, the pin wouldn't have pricked anywhere near Älggialp.

In fact, something utterly shocking happens when you do put mountains on the cardboard. The highest mountains in Switzerland, in Valais, pull the center of gravity to the southwest. At the same time, the large mountainous territory of Graubünden pulls to the east-southeast. The Graubünden mountains, which stretch further away from Älggi than the Valaisan do, compensate with their greater lever arm for their lower mass—and the center of Switzerland moves distinctly to the south-southeast. According to my calculations, in fact, it moves to the point with Swiss coordinates 677106/145155.

The real center of Switzerland is not at Älggialp, but at a place called Alpe Regina. It's a relatively flat area, at an altitude of about 2,230 meters, and the triangulation pyramid could be placed on the exact spot, not 500 meters away. Everything would be hunky-dory.

Except for one problem. There would be no place to prick the pin.

Alpe Regina is in Italy.[2] The center of Switzerland is ruled by Rome.

---

2   Physically, this is a perfectly reasonable result. The center of gravity of an object is often located outside the object itself—that of a coffee mug, for example, is in the empty space inside the mug.

45

How Much Vacation Do You Get If You're Unemployed in Switzerland?

Being unemployed is hard work in Switzerland. You have to meet every month with a counselor to brainstorm and discuss your prospects. You have to submit a certain number of applications every month to potential employers; you submit these to your counselor as well. If your counselor thinks fit, she'll send you to a course to beef up your job qualifications, or a coach to help you write your cover letters and CVs. The course or coach fees are covered, and you get reimbursed for any transportation costs. You may also be working at part-time or irregular jobs while you're looking for your next real job.

All work and no play, however, makes Johnny a dull boy. So unemployed people get four weeks of paid vacation every year—vacation from being unemployed. You clear it with your counselor two weeks in advance, and have to take at least five days off at a time. You can save up your vacation time from year to year.

Every employee in Switzerland pays a monthly premium for unemployment insurance, which is deducted from his or her salary. When unemployment strikes, it's treated like an illness or an accident: the insurance pays until you get better, and the counselor acts as your doctor—for up to two years. You receive 80 percent of your last salary.

Only after two years of unsuccessful job applications do you move to another system—that of state administered social assistance.

In many countries, taking a paid vacation from being unemployed would raise eyebrows. In Switzerland it's the unremarkable norm.

46

Who is Switzerland's Most Beloved Criminal?

He broke out of prison in Sion twice in two years. The first time he put the jailor out of action by tossing a plate of hot polenta in his face; the second time he used a saw constructed from a woman's corset to remove the bars of his cell. When he broke out of jail in Ivrea, Italy, it was the jailor's own daughter who snuck him enough wool to braid the rope he climbed down to freedom.

"We were fascinated by him," remembered a man from Riddes, "especially when he emerged from the pub. People waited on the streets for him. He shouldered his gun and his bag and as he walked off he tossed out his coins. I was still a small boy back then, but I will never forget it." More than a century after his death, the Bishop of Sion declined to attend a performance of a play about him "out of fear that the beautiful image that my parents passed on of him might somehow be diluted."

Valais in the 19th century was an impoverished area. Most of the people were subsistence farmers, scraping out a living from miserable hovels. The Rhône river was unchanneled and coursed as it wished through the swampy valley floor, a haven for fugitives from all over Europe, a breeding ground for malaria and crime. The soil of the mountains, lacking in iodine, produced a population plagued by goiters and cretinism. And in 1870 the Valaisan Cantonal Bank collapsed.

Enter Joseph Samuel Farinet. From his hideouts, with his gangs and his know-how, he began producing and distributing 20-centime pieces dated 1850. So many and so successfully that at one point over a third of the coinage circulating in Valais stemmed from his workshop. *Farinet's money is better than the state's,* the people said—and, considering the bank catastrophe, it was true. The gratitude and sympathy of the poor Valaisans allowed Farinet to play cat-and-mouse with the law for well over a decade.

In March, 1878, however, the cat finally caught up with the mice. Farinet's accomplices were hauled into court, their dismantled embossing machine was found dumped in a river, and Farinet himself was on the run.

He ran. For two years, wanted on both sides of the border, he made fools of the police, of the politicians, of the entire Swiss state. He slept in mountain huts and under the stars; he slept in barns and in the houses of the many people sympathetic to him; he slept with the lovers who fed and cared for him. He showed up in pubs and drank the wine he loved and played his fiddle, showered his coins on the people, and always vanished just before the *gendarmes* arrived. A bounty of 400 francs was set on his head; soon it was doubled.

Farinet became a living legend. Relations between Switzerland and Italy deteriorated over the Swiss failure to apprehend him, and the Swiss Federal Council sent urgent messages to the Valaisan government—*Catch this man!* The Department of Justice of Valais made it a crime even to mention his name.

And then one day in April, 1880, his whereabouts were betrayed by a jealous lover. The net drew tight. Farinet escaped to a gorge near Saillon, but there he was trapped. Scrambling about on the cliffs above the Salentse river, dodging bullets fired by the police from the other side, he ran out of food and water.

On the 17th of April, 1880, he stumbled off the cliff into the gorge. Or was shot through the head and fell in. Or committed suicide. No one knows. The pathologist who performed the autopsy found only one thing in his otherwise empty stomach: a wild violet.[1]

Then only the legend lived on. In 1932 the Swiss author C.F. Ramuz wrote the novel *Farinet*; Max Haufler directed the 1939 film *Or dans la montagne*, with soundtrack by the distinguished Swiss composer Arthur Honegger. In 1980, 100 actors resurrected Farinet's legend in an outdoor production on the rooftops of Sion, between the prison and the cathedral. When the Swiss adventurer Bertrand Piccard took off from Château-d'Oex in 1999 to make the first nonstop balloon trip around the world, he had one of Farinet's coins in his pocket. In a country notable for the absence of statues commemorating its heroes, that of Farinet in Saillon joined that of William Tell in Altdorf. Tell was a hero fighting foreign oppression; Farinet gave away money to combat domestic injustice.

---

1   You might ask, if there was a pathologist performing an autopsy, why don't we know if there was a bullet in his head? The answer is that the police would not have wanted to be seen as having shot him, and the pathologist, who said there was no bullet, may have lied.

The *Amis de Farinet* established the *Vineyard of Peace* in his honor; it is owned by the Dalai Lama, who has come to harvest its grapes, and is the smallest registered vineyard in the world. Pilgrims to this living shrine have brought rocks from the Cheops Pyramid, the Acropolis, Ephesus, Machu Picchu, Montmartre, the Berlin Wall, Easter Island, Delphi, Mount Sinai, Mecca and Ayers Rock to line its ground. Besides the Dalai Lama, celebrities such as Zinedine Zidane, Gina Lollobrigida, Michael Schumacher, Ben Kingsley, Roger Moore and the Abbé Pierre have come to Saillon to pick the grapes; in 1992 Philippe Petit walked a 300-meter tightrope to the harvest. Diluted with wines from other vineyards, 1,000 bottles of *Farinet* are annually auctioned off at prices that reach 500 francs, with the proceeds going to cultural and charitable causes. The Farinet Path to the vineyard, adorned with stained glass sculptures by Robert Héritier and Théo Imboden, has become a pilgrimage site for free spirits.

"Freedom, it exists," says Ramuz's Farinet, on the run in the mountains, "and you place it on your medals and your coins; but here with me is the thing itself; she is sitting right beside me."

Today Farinet's story has come full circle. In May, 2017, the *Association Le Farinet* launched a complementary local currency in Valais: the *Farinet*. Bills have been issued in denominations of 1, 5, 10, 13,[2] 20, 50, and 100 *Farinets*. Over 150 businesses in Valais will now accept *Farinets* in lieu of francs.

Which forces a rather lovely question on us. What if someone were, in the spirit of Farinet, to counterfeit *Farinets?* Would anybody dare complain?

---

2   There are 13 stars on the Valaisan flag, representing the 13 districts in the canton.

47

If a Hostile Country Wanted to Attack Switzerland, What Would Be the Best Way to Do It?

On February 17th, 2014, the pilot of an Ethiopian Air 767 heading to Rome needed to use the restroom. While he was out of the cockpit, the co-pilot locked the door and took over the controls. His goal was to land in Geneva and seek asylum there.[1]

The hijacked plane was escorted by Italian Eurofighter jets over Italy. French Mirage fighters took over the escort above France and continued it right into Swiss airspace. The plane landed in Geneva, where the co-pilot climbed out of the cockpit window, shimmied down a rope and turned himself in to the waiting police.

---

1   Instead of asylum he initially got a diagnosis of paranoid schizophrenia and was sentenced to hospitalization and therapy. Switzerland didn't comply with Ethiopia's request to extradite him to serve the 19-year sentence he had been handed there in absentia, and in 2016 his asylum request was granted.

The Swiss Air Force didn't take over the escort from the French because it was 6:00 in the morning and their pilots didn't start work until 8:00. It wouldn't have been able to take over the escort after 17:00, either, because that's when the Swiss Air Force pilots packed up and went home.

Switzerland may be a landlocked country, but 472 kilometers of its border comes in liquid form. As we learned in Question 4, the Swiss Navy does its training right in the middle of the country, on Lake Luzern. Naval shows employing the entire fleet occasionally take place there as well.

Combining these two facts, the strategy for an attack is obvious: a naval attack at night at a time when the Swiss patrol boats are all on Lake Luzern. Think of it: who's going to suspect a *naval* attack on Switzerland? Your spies will want to notice when all fourteen of Motorboat Company 10's new patrol boats are training or parading in the middle of the country. Then, under cover of darkness and outside of the Air Force's office hours—which today run until 18:00[2]—you'll want to launch a four-pronged attack on Lakes Constance, Geneva, Maggiore and Lugano. Four warships with amphibious landing craft will sail across the borders and unload your troops. There will be no patrol boats to stop you, and you'll be guaranteed safety from the air until at least 8 a.m. In fact, if you can throw an aircraft carrier into the mix, you'll be able to take out the airfields at Payerne, Emmen, Sion, Locarno, Meiringen and Alpnach before dawn, and you won't have to worry about the Air Force at all.

---

2   Except on Mondays. Don't do this on a Monday.

You'll want to do this soon, though. Already in 2019 the Swiss Air Force is going to have pilots on call from 6:00 to 22:00. This would only give you 8 hours to launch the attack, rather than the current 14.

After 2021, forget it. By then the Air Force will have launched Project *Luftpolizeidienst 24*—Air Police Service 24—and there will be two (2) pilots sleeping near jets at the airfield in Payerne every night of the year, ready to fly within fifteen minutes of an alarm.

At this point you might as well pack up and go home yourself.

48

What Was Switzerland Like During the last Ice Age? Will it Ever Be That Way Again?

24,000 years ago Switzerland looked like a huge dome of ice with just the tops of the highest peaks sticking out of it. Only the top half of the Matterhorn's north face, for example, would have been seen jutting out of a massive ice plateau. This demi-Matterhorn would have been invisible from Zermatt, had Zermatt existed, because Zermatt's current location was buried under a kilometer and a half of ice.

But not only Zermatt. Even gentle Geneva lay under 800 meters of frozen water.

To picture how deep this is, imagine that an angry god was dumping ice cubes on Manhattan. The ice cubes pile up as they pelt down, filling in the streets, burying the streetlamps, climbing up the sides of the skyscrapers. At a certain point, the great heap of ice cubes reaches the top of the highest buildings, and Manhattan, viewed from the air, is just a big frozen mound. The angry god keeps hurling ice, however, until the pile is *twice* as high as the Empire State Building. That's how deeply Geneva was buried.

And that was relatively little. Sion and Chur lay under twice as much ice as Geneva. A loaded 747, if it could take off from Sion today, would take about 3 minutes to clear the level of that ancient glacier's surface.

This huge dome of ice didn't rise up to a single summit, however. It was instead composed of three different domes-within-the-dome: one, the Rhône Dome, summited 1,600 meters above today's Oberwald; the second, the Vorderrhein Dome, peaked 1,800m above Disentis; and the third and highest of all, the Engadiner Dome, topped off at over 3,000 meters above sea level, some 1,300 meters above St. Moritz. The ice extended to the south well into Italy (Domodossola lay under a kilometer and a half of it), and to the west well into France. In the northwest the icecap ended near the Jura mountains, though a peninsula of tundra poking into the Emmental managed to stay clear. To the east the glaciers covered most of Austria, finally ending at today's Klagenfurt near the Slovenian border.

That's probably the answer you were looking for, but it's not the right one. Using the correct scientific terminology, the answer is in fact completely different. So let's try it again. What was Switzerland like during the last ice age?

Well, have a look.

That's right—Switzerland, and the entire planet, is still in the *middle* of an ice age—the world's fifth. It's known as the Pliocene Quaternary Ice Age, and began around 2.6 million years ago—about the time Homo Habilus, the first animal of our own genus, was developing in Africa.

An ice age is defined as a period in which there are permanent continental (e.g., Greenland) and polar (e.g., Antarctica) ice sheets, as well as glaciers in the mountains. For much of our planet's natural history, this has not been the case, but it is the case today. The earth will emerge from the current ice age only when the Antarctic, Greenland and the Himalayas have lost their frozen blankets, and most of our coastal cities are under water.

The picture I sketched above of Switzerland under its great triple dome of ice described what is known as the Last Glacial Maximum (or LGM). Since the withdrawal of the glaciers from the Alpine valleys about 12,000 years ago, we have been in what is called an *inter*glacial period *within* an ice age. Ours is known as the Holocene.

Yet even within an interglacial period like the Holocene the ice advances and retreats. A "Little Ice Age"—a *glacial* maximum within an *interglacial* period—marked the years between 1300 and 1850. Engravings and paintings of Switzerland from that time show dramatically thicker and longer glaciers than you will see today, and we can still easily read the signs, in the form of high moraines and sculpted rock surfaces, that speak of the significantly greater extent of the ice just a few centuries ago. In the early 1700s the people of Grindelwald, alarmed at the advance of the Upper Grindelwald Glacier into their meadows, hired an exorcist in an attempt to force it back. The trick appeared to work, for the glacier stopped advancing.

And the future? Yes, Switzerland will probably be covered in ice again. In the normal course of things, glacial and interglacial periods alternate every forty to one hundred thousand years—driven by a number of factors, such as the varying orbit of the earth and the changeable burning of the sun.

Human-caused global warming may delay the next glacial maximum, but will hardly stop it from coming. The damage we are causing to the environment that supports us may hasten our extinction—but in the grand scheme of things, nature's far more powerful processes will shrug at the effects of our civilization, and carry on doing their thing, as they always have.

49

What Would Happen if a Dam Broke?

There are detailed maps illustrating the flow of water after the bursting of major Swiss dams. Most of these maps are top secret. The official reason given for the secrecy is that terrorists might use the information to foul ends.

This reason is less than convincing. The likelihood that terrorists could break up a Swiss dam is vanishingly small. The more likely reason is that the consequences of a burst dam are too terrifying for the mental health of the affected populations. For Zurich, Chur and Sion—all capital cities that lie below major dams—ignorance may be bliss. "We don't give out certain data," says Claude-Alain Roch, director of the civil protection department of Valais, and justifies this secrecy with the wish not to incite unnecessary fears. He adds that "living in a town near the Grande Dixence dam is like living next door to a nuclear power plant."

Even without the maps, however, we can come up with some reasonably likely scenarios.

The Grand Dixence is, at 285 meters, the tallest concrete dam in the world—just a few meters short of the Eiffel tower. Behind its wall lurk some 400,000,000 *tons* of water. Should the dam break apart, this water would head down the Val d'Hérémence and then the Val d'Hérens, laying both waste. Half an hour after the collapse, a 35-meter-high wall of water would strike Sion, the capital city of Valais, and utterly destroy it. The waters would spread out as they rampaged down the Rhône valley, taking out Saxon, Martigny, St. Maurice, Bex, and Aigle before running into Lake Geneva. The sudden surge of water into the lake would create a tsunami that would head west, destroying lakeside towns in both Switzerland and France, much of Lausanne, and finally hitting Geneva. Geneva would vanish (see Questions 2 and 9).

Presumably the collapse of the dam would be noticed by workers above it and an alarm would be sent out. Emergency sirens would sound in Sion; people would turn on their radios and be instructed to get to high ground. Those on foot might race up the lanes and paths of the two hills that romantically dominate the city, topped by a ruined castle and a great basilica. The tops of these hills are 150 meters above the rest of the city. This might be safe. Or, with the surge crashing up the slopes, it might not.

Those in cars would find themselves desperately fighting their way through traffic to reach a high enough spot in the vineyards on the northern side of the city. Many would be stuck too low as the swell hit.

No wonder the maps are top secret.

A tiny preview of this devastation was given us on December 13th, 2000. A shaft carrying water from the Grand Dixence toward the Bieudron turbines in Nendaz burst, releasing

50,000 tons of water traveling at 690 kilometers per hour at almost 200 times atmospheric pressure. Seventeen houses were swept down to the valley, and three people lost their lives. The amount of water released was one eight-thousandth of the amount that would be loosed in a full-fledged catastrophe.

The likelihood of a dam break at the Dixence is very small. The dam consists of six million cubic meters of concrete, which translates into fourteen and a half *billion* kilograms. If we were to try to use up this much concrete building a wall—a wall 10 centimeters thick and 1.5 meters high—we could start in Quito, Ecuador, and head due east. We would cross Columbia and Brazil, and hardly have made a dent in our supply. We would keep on building it all the way across the Atlantic Ocean,[1] then Gabon, Congo, Democratic Republic of Congo, Uganda, Kenya, Soa Tome and Principe, and Somalia. Our supply of concrete would be noticeably smaller at this point, but still substantial. We would cross the Indian Ocean, Maldives, Indonesia, the Pacific Ocean, Kiribati, more Pacific Ocean. We would eventually use up all of the Grand Dixence's concrete, but not until we got to . . . Quito again! Once around the equator—we're talking about a lot of concrete here.

The Grande Dixence dam is *two hundred meters thick* at its base, which is almost inconceivable—a wall, two football-pitch lengths *thick*. It thins out to 15 meters at its crest. This crest is over 700 meters long. *Inside* the dam are hidden 15 *kilometers* of tunnels, and as many again of shafts and lifts.

The tunnels inside the wall are damp, with water dripping from their ceilings. This is because the dam *leaks*—to the tune

---

1   Yes, this might be problematic, I know.

of 7 liters per second, rising to 12 liters per second when the reservoir is full.

Not only does the concrete leak—it also sways. The crest of the dam moves back and forth up to eleven centimeters, depending on the amount of water in the reservoir.

The Grande Dixence is a gravity dam. What holds the wall in place is not a powerful superglue sticking it to the mountainside. No, it's simply too heavy for anything to budge it— even 400,000,000 tons of backed-up water.

As you can see, terrorists would have a pretty hard time with this thing. At its weakest point, it's a 15-meter thick concrete wall. If you were surrounded by a 15-meter thick concrete wall, I think you'd feel pretty safe—from anything. Let the bombs fly.

As Henri Pougatsch of the Federal Office of Water and Geology said when asked how long the dam would last: "How long have the pyramids been around?"[2]

In fact, the only thing that would seem to have a chance against this dam would be a natural catastrophe of great magnitude. As, say, an earthquake. And you can be sure that the careful Swiss have not built the tallest gravity dam in the world in an earthquake zone! In fact, to reassure myself, I was happy to find an *unclassified* map that has a bearing on this question: a map that shows where seismic activity has occurred in Swit-

---

2   Like the pyramids, the Dixence took a toll on human life. Sixty construction workers died in accidents, avalanches, and through too much drink. The worksheds at the 2360-meter-high construction site stored coffins at the ready—and workers, after tippling, sometimes slept in them as a joke. Thousands are thought to have died of silicosis after the dam's completion. (See Question 3.)

Among the construction workers was a 23-year-old French-Swiss man named Jean-Luc Godard, who would later become one of the leading French New Wave film directors. Godard spent his earnings on a movie camera, got himself moved from construction work to running the switchboard, and made his first movie—*Operation Béton (Operation Concrete)*—at the Grand Dixence.

zerland over the years. I just wanted to double check. Not that I had any real doubts—but, it can't hurt, right?

I noted happily that the Grand Dixence is located right next to the reddest zone in Switzerland, down in the lower left part of the map. Red means "stop," so I figured this meant a zone that earthquakes never get to. Pretty good, right? Pretty safe. Those careful Swiss engineers think of everything!

Except . . . hmm. I'm looking at the key now. I'm looking at what red means . . .

Never mind.

Maybe they should classify this map too.

50

How Will the Swiss Ski Industry Die?

The problems for the Swiss ski industry induced by global warming will be many and varied, according to the Swiss Federal Office of Political Economy:

In the future the number of snow-secure areas will decrease dramatically in certain regions. Other aspects relevant to tourism include: absence of a winter atmosphere, no snow in the Swiss plateau, a collapse of demand, a lack of water for making artificial snow, costly investment for artificial snow and for the reservoirs required to make it, a shorter season because of later snow in the fall and earlier melting in the spring, a reduction in ideal ski days due to less sun and more frequent strong winds, the search for new locations for ski-schools, a shift to higher altitudes, challenges in the face of natural disasters, an imperiled infrastructure due to the melting of permafrost, and floods and washouts.

This does not bode well. Dozens of small ski areas have already shut down in Switzerland, especially at lower altitudes. Climate physicist Reto Knutti of the ETH says:

If we assume a moderate emissions scenario, by the end of the century the snow season will be shorter by four to eight weeks. The snow level will lie 500 to 700 meters higher than it does today. For all ski areas at intermediate altitudes— that is, between 1000 and 2000 meters—things will become very problematic.

Furthermore, Knutti adds, "Of course artificial snow is of some help. But when it's too warm, that doesn't work either. You can't change the laws of physics."

Switzerland has some 39 major groups of ski areas—many of which are agglomerations of previously independent resorts. The vast majority of their ski trails are between 1000 and 2000 meters. Many will die out. The higher ski areas, which are concentrated in Valais and Graubünden, may survive—as a much more exotic and exclusive playground—but even most of them will lose their lower slopes.

If that weren't all bad enough, here's Reto Knutti with a Swiss particularity:

Seen historically, the temperature increase in Switzerland has been about double the world average—worldwide one degree since preindustrial times, but in Switzerland two.[1]

---

1   This may be due partly to the melting of the glaciers and the earlier melting of snow in the spring. The snow and ice melt because the air is warmer and the air then gets warmer because it's not cooled by the snow and ice. A vicious loop.

* * *

Switzerland survived for most of its history without skiing—only in 1889 did the Branger brothers of Davos begin teaching themselves the sport in secret, with Norwegian skis they had purchased in Paris.[2] The first tourist on skis was Sherlock Holmes's creator, Arthur Conan Doyle, who accompanied his wife to Davos for a tuberculosis cure, found out about the Brangers, and convinced them to include him in the game. Doyle wrote:

> There is nothing peculiarly malignant in the appearance of a pair of skis. They are two slips of elm wood, eight feet long, four inches broad, with a square heel, turned-up toes, and straps in the centre to secure your feet. No one, to look at them, would guess at the possibilities which lurk in them. But you put them on and you turn with a smile to see whether your friends are looking at you, and then the next moment you are boring your head madly into a snow bank, and kicking frantically with both feet, and half-rising, only to butt viciously into that snow bank again, and your friends are getting more entertainment than they had ever thought you capable of giving.

The Brangers and Doyle skied without a ski resort. The extinction of ski areas doesn't have to mean the extinction of skiing—only of what Doyle's compatriot, the Himalayan climber Frank Smythe, dubbed "downhill-only skiing" in

---

2   The first recorded descent in Switzerland was by the Valaisan minister Johann Joseph Imseng from Saas Fee to Saas Grund, in 1849. It didn't catch on then, however, and the beginning of the phenomenon "Skiing in Switzerland" is credited to the Brangers.

1934—the year the world's first T-bar was constructed in Davos. According to Smythe, the extinction of resorts would be of great benefit to the world:

Skiing in other people's grooves is a useful discipline for commercial routine, and it produces a type without which the dictators of this world would have to go out of business.

If Smythe is right, we may be looking not at a disaster, but at the solution to many of our woes.

Switzerland can be happy about one thing. Its ski areas are generally located at higher altitudes than Alpine neighbor Austria's. If Swiss skiing goes down the tubes, Austria's will have preceded it—increasing demand and raising prices in Valais and Graubünden. Some Swiss ski areas might even limp along for quite a long time. The middle-class skier, however, is definitely an endangered species.

51

How Much Rubble was Excavated Building the World's Longest Tunnel? And Where Is It Now?

The world's longest tunnel, at 127 kilometers, is the Delaware Aqueduct, which supplies New York City with its water and so doesn't belong in this book. But let's answer the question for the longest *traffic* tunnel—the newly completed Gotthard Base Tunnel in Switzerland.

We could answer in cubic meters (13.3 million) or metric tons (28.2 million), but nobody except an engineer will be able to make much of such measures. So let's answer in freight cars, and say that if you were to load all of the rubble on a single train, that train would stretch in a straight line from Zurich to Kathmandu.

Of course, there are no straight tracks leading from Zurich to Kathmandu. So if we actually want to transport all this rubble to the Himalayas, it's going to cost us some trouble. As far as I can tell by studying rail maps, our train could go, via

Moscow, Turkmenistan, and Tehran, to a place called Sibi Junction in Pakistan, but at this point we'd run out of track. We'd have to lay down some 500 kilometers of rails to take us to Jakhal, in western India. From there we could pick up an existing line to New Delhi, and from New Delhi we could get to Gorakhpur. From here we'd have to lay down another 200 kilometers of track to get to Kathmandu.

Furthermore, there's the problem of how to move 28 million tons of train. The BLS tells me that two of their locomotives will pull up to 2,000 tons through the Lötschberg Base Tunnel; extrapolating from this we'd need 28,000 locomotives to get this baby moving. That's a line of locomotives 560 *kilometers* long, and is 400 times as many as the Swiss Federal Railway owns. So we'd have to borrow from all over Europe—and beyond—causing massive problems in public transportation throughout the world. But there'd be massive problems anyway, since we're occupying so damned much track—over 6,000 kilometers—before we even start moving. And we haven't even considered other problems, such as varying gauges of track and the strength of the couplings between the cars, which would be nowhere near up to this job.

This is starting to seem like a very bad idea. And disposing of this rubble is starting to look like a very complicated problem. What to do?

Luckily, there was a second problem with this tunnel, and the two problems solved each other.

You see, 80 percent of the Gotthard Base Tunnel was drilled out by four sisters named Heidi, Sissi, Gabi 1 and Gabi 2. These sisters are TBMs—Tunnel Boring Machines. They're tough as nails—actually, far, far tougher. 62 disc cutters mounted on a spinning cutterhead rotate against the rock with a pressure of

32 tons each, while hydraulic gripper plates press the cutter-head forward by seizing onto the already excavated tunnel walls behind. 10 motors per machine use up 63 megawatt-hours of electricity per day—the amount of energy used by 4,200 households. And that's only one TBM. Each one of them is over 400 meters long, almost six times as long as a 747; seen from the side they look like a kind of huge mechanical tad-pole, a nightmare from a Star Wars battle.

The cutterheads are round, and make a round hole in the rock—a circle with a diameter of 9.58 meters. And this brings us to the second problem I mentioned above: trains need flat, not round, surfaces for their tracks. And there's even a third problem: as you might have guessed from the description so far of Sissi and Co., they're not exactly into interior decora-tion. They left a pretty damned rugged hole in that mountain. So that hole had to be smoothed over with concrete.

Something had to be done. We needed fill to flatten the bottom of the tunnel, and we needed 2 million cubic meters of concrete to make the tunnel smooth. Where were we going to get all that fill, and all that concrete?

What we needed was some rubble.

And so the problems solved each other: we needed rubble—and boy, did we have rubble. Thirty-three percent of the exca-vated rock was processed into concrete to line the tunnel, and 7 percent went back as fill. In fact, all of the concrete used in the entire tunnel was made from excavated stone.

Henry David Thoreau wrote that, "Most men would feel in-sulted if it were proposed to employ them in throwing stones over a wall, and then in throwing them back, merely that they might earn their wages." But of course, the tunnel builders didn't just *throw* the stones back. The ones used to make concrete had to be carefully selected and processed, since not all rock makes good concrete. But that was okay, because there sure was plenty of rock to choose from.

In fact, after all the necessary rubble had been put back *into* the tunnel to level and prettify it, there was still some 16 *million* tons to dispose of.

What to do with 16 million tons of rubble? We've already ruled out shipping it to Kathmandu. But here's another idea: how about building a few islands, and shoring up a badly eroded delta?

Yes, six new islands were built in nearby Lake Uri with debris from the Gotthard excavation. Three of them make up a wilderness preserve, and now serve as home to over 200 different varieties of birds and numerous endangered species of amphibians and fish. The other three islands serve as swimming beaches—a little Caribbean in central Switzerland. And the Reuss delta, which had been badly depleted by a century of gravel harvesting, and was plagued by flooding and land loss, has been shored up again.

Um—gravel harvesting? That's right. For a century people took gravel *away* from the Reuss delta. And yes, now they're putting gravel back. What was it that Thoreau was saying?

After the islands and the delta there was still some rubble left, but it was sold as fill and gravel. Only 0.7 percent of the excavated material went to waste.

That's what we call recycling—on a grand scale.

52

Is Switzerland Homophobic?

On May 6th, 2018, a young politician from the CVP (Christian Democratic People's Party) tweeted that it had been almost 15 years since the Swiss sovereign (see Question 7) approved same-sex civil unions, and quoted a former federal councilor who had noted that "the time is ripe for discussing further measures to promote equality."

In response to this tweet, Christian Ineichen, an older CVP politician, himself tweeted "And: we should stay within the limits of biology, and acknowledge its providence."

On being asked to specify what exactly he intended by this statement, Ineichen tweeted:

> Man + Woman: okay.
> Woman + Woman: somehow okay.
> Man + Man: not okay.

This Tweet led to what the online news service *Watson* called a "severe shitstorm" breaking over Ineichen. One of the most pointed tweets in response read, "Dear Mr. Ineichen, If all went according to the providence of biology, after your last heart attack you would have been dead."[1]

On the Ilga (International Gay, Lesbian, Bisexual, Trans and Intersex Association) Rainbow Europe map for 2017, Switzerland got mediocre marks, fulfilling only 31 percent of the criteria for full legal equality, and ranking 26th out of the 49 countries evaluated—right in the middle. If Ilga were to model a tweet after Ineichen's, it might look something like this:

Malta (at 86 percent, top of the list): okay
Switzerland: somehow okay
Azerbaijan (at 5 percent, bottom of list): not okay

A second tweet from Ilga might analyze Switzerland's score in more depth:

Civil society space (freedom of association, expression, events): okay
Equality and nondiscrimination: somehow okay
Hate crime and hate speech: not okay

Switzerland fails in the hate crime and hate speech category because it currently fulfills exactly *zero* of Ilga's eight criteria. And precisely because Switzerland doesn't have laws forbidding homophobic or transphobic remarks or violence (as it does, for example, for racially, ethnically or religiously motivated hate speech and crime), there are very few statistics that describe the extent of Swiss homophobia. The most meaningful come from the *Santé gaie* project in Geneva, a collaboration

---

1   Although it could easily be interpreted otherwise, Ineichen's tweet was ostensibly directed to family constellations rather than sexual activities.

between the Genevan association *Dialogai* and the University of Zurich, and they only deal with gay men.

To get a handle on the *Santé gaie* numbers, we can imagine a country called Quitzerland, with the same population and the same laws as Switzerland, but the interesting characteristic that all of Quitzerland's 8.5 million residents are gay men. No children, no women, no straight males. None of these men would be married—though a small fraction, about 550,000, would be living in registered partnerships.[2] (In Switzerland, meanwhile, about 3.5 million people are married.) A registered partnership between a citizen and a foreign resident would not make it any easier for the foreign partner to get a passport, however. Nor would the couple be allowed to jointly adopt children.[3] In this, Quitzerland would be not much different if it were inhabited by lesbians—except that the number of registered partnerships would only be about half as high.

But now comes the heavy stuff. Extrapolating from the *Sainté gaie* statistics, Quitzerland, with its population of 8.5 million, would be home to over 6 million victims of some form of violence. (This is 3–4 times the number for Switzerland.) In addition, 1.4 million residents would at some point in their lives have attempted suicide. Almost a million of those attempts would have been made before the age of 20. Quitzerland would

---

2   There is little hard data to base these extrapolations on—the number of homosexuals in Switzerland is unknown, and there is no agreed upon definition of homosexual, either. Sainté gaie estimates that 3 percent of the adult population is gay, and feel-ok.ch puts it at between 3 and 10 percent. I've used a figure of 5 percent. The adult population of Switzerland is around 7 million, so that makes about 350,000 gay and lesbian adults; if we figure half of these are men, we come to 175,000. To populate the entire country we would have to multiply by about 50. There are about 11,000 gay men living in registered partnerships in Switzerland today—multiplying by 50 gives us 550,000 men in registered partnerships in Quitzerland.

3   Paradoxically, single men or women who have *not* registered a partnership *could* adopt children.

have, by far, the highest teen suicide rate of any country in the world.[4]

In 2019 the Swiss parliament will debate proposed legislation both on gay marriage and on extending the anti-discrimination law to cover LGBTI hate crimes. Both measures are supported by the overwhelming majority of Swiss citizens: a 2016 poll by the gay men's organization Pink Cross showed almost 70 percent in favor of same-sex marriage—including 56 percent of the right-wing Swiss People's Party (SVP)—and 86 percent in favor of criminalizing anti-LGBTI hate speech and violence. If the politicians follow the polls, Switzerland's spot in the Ilga rankings will soon change—in the direction of "okay." If this helps to reduce Swiss gay teen suicide attempts, that would probably be "okay" too—in almost anybody's tweet.

---

4   This is four to five times the overall Swiss rate. The *Santé gaie* statistics come from a sample of gay men in the Geneva area rather than the whole of Switzerland. The dramatic rate of attempted suicide is consistent with data from other countries, however, so there is no reason to believe that Geneva represents a Swiss anomaly.

53

Are the Swiss Alps Growing or Shrinking?

Both.

The Alps shrink because of erosion. Wind, water, glaciers and rockfall are constantly removing material from the tops of the mountains and sending it down to the valleys.

In 1871 Edward Whymper, one of the two men to first set foot on the summit of the Matterhorn (see Question 32), described the forces of erosion on that mountain.[1] He was responding to John Ruskin, the English art critic and mountain lover, who had called the Matterhorn "indestructible."

> *"There is no aspect of destruction about the Matterhorn cliffs," says Professor Ruskin. Granted—when they are seen from afar. But approach, and sit down by the side of the Z'Muttgletscher, and you will hear that their piecemeal destruction is proceeding ceaselessly—incessantly. You will hear, but, probably, you will not see; for even when the de-*

---

1 Whymper and the Chamonix guide Michel Croz were the first two of their party of seven to reach the summit. They unroped some dozens of meters before the top and "ran a neck-and-neck race" that ended in a "dead heat."

scending masses thunder as loudly as heavy guns, and the echoes roll back from the Ebihorn opposite, they will still be pin-points against the grand old face, so vast is its scale!

If you would see the "aspects of destruction," you must come still closer, and climb its cliffs and ridges, or mount to the plateau of the Matterhorngletscher, which is cut up and ploughed by these missiles, and strewn on the surface with their smaller fragments. The larger masses, falling with tremendous velocity, plunge into the snow and are lost to sight.

So much for erosion. But why are the Alps simultaneously growing? You might think that the collision of tectonic plates that gave rise (literally) to the Alps millions of years ago is still ongoing, but you'd be wrong—while the Alps *are* a young mountain range, the Alpine area has been "dead" tectonically for some time now.[2]

And yet they grow. To picture the surprising cause, imagine you have a suitcase full of rocks sitting on a trampoline. The suitcase rises above the surface of the trampoline, but at the same time presses down on it.

If you were now to take the rocks out of the suitcase, but place them on the trampoline right near it, you wouldn't see much difference in the height of the top of the suitcase, because the rocks would still be pressing down the trampoline.

If, however, instead of filling it with rocks, you were to place a large block of ice on top of the suitcase, things would start to happen. Imagine that the ice is in a lightweight plastic tub with a hose running out of the bottom of it and leading off the trampoline. As the ice melts, the weight on the trampoline decreases because the water flows out of the system. Gradually,

---

2   Except for certain parts of Austria, where the circular motion of the Adriatic subplate is still providing a tectonic contribution to the landscape.

the trampoline will be become less and less compressed, and the top of the suitcase will rise.

Now you have to imagine a very, very slowly rebounding trampoline, by which I mean one that holds the impression of a weight on it for a long time after that weight has actually disappeared. Since there are no very slow trampolines, think instead of a carpet that has had a table sitting on it for years. When you take away the table, the impressions of the table's feet remain. Eventually these compressed spots will rise up and the carpet will level out, but those dents in the carpet will often remain long after the table has been carried away.

Twenty-four thousand years ago, at the time of the Last Glacial Maximum (see Question 48), the Alps were a suitcase full of rocks with a block of ice on top. The rocks represent rocks, while the block of ice is the huge glacial dome that partly covered them. The trampoline itself is the earth's crust, which got compressed under all of that weight.

When the mountains erode, the rocks they lose end up in the valleys. From there they continue to compress the earth's crust as much as they did when they were at the top of the peaks—just as the rocks that were placed around the suitcase compressed the trampoline as much as when they were in it. But the massive amounts of ice—62,000 gigatons[3]—that covered the mountains 24,000 years ago melted and *didn't* stick around, but flowed out to the oceans. The earth's crust reacts VERY SLOWLY to this loss of weight, and is still decompressing today—like the carpet that had the foot of the table imprinted in it. This decompression of the crust lifts up the Alps just as the decompression of the trampoline lifted up the suitcase.

---

3   That's 62,000,000,000,000,000 kilos, or close to 10 million kilos for every person alive today.

*　*　*

The decompression of the earth's crust, which "grows" the Alps, and the work of erosion, which "shrinks" them, almost completely balance each other out. Overall, the rising crust is slightly winning out over the falling boulders, and the Alps are gaining in height very slightly, to the tune of about a millimeter a year. Despite this, however, they still aren't as high as they were several million years ago. Their current growth is, geologically speaking, a short-term reaction to the glacial melting since the last LGM, rather than the continuation of a long-term trend.

54

How Happy Are the Swiss?

The UN Sustainable Development Solutions Network puts out a *World Happiness Report* every year. It's based on the following question, known as the Cantril Ladder Question:

> *Please imagine a ladder, with steps numbered from 0 at the bottom to 10 at the top. The top of the ladder represents the best possible life for you and the bottom of the ladder represents the worst possible life for you. On which step of the ladder would you say you personally feel you stand at this time?*

The 2014–2016 Swiss score of 7.494 came in fourth place behind Norway's, Denmark's and Iceland's, and just ahead of Finland's. The differences in the top five scores are statistically insignificant, however, so it's justifiable to say that the Swiss, along with the residents of those four Nordic countries, are the happiest people in the world. And have been for many years.

Or not. There are of course other interpretations of the Cantril score. Saying that I'm standing on the top rung of the ladder might not mean that I'm happy. It might simply mean, I'm pleased with my station in life. I'm satisfied with my position. Look at me: I'm doing great.

Has the UN, perhaps, produced a World *Smug Self-Satisfaction Report*?

One of the reasons the authors of the report choose to use the Cantril Ladder Question is that the life evaluations it elicits vary far more between countries than emotional states do. This makes for a report that packs more punch—especially when thinking about policy. But is it happiness? Here is a Happiness Report pollster in 2015, when the Swiss topped the ranking outright:[1]

> *It just depends on how you define happiness. If you think happiness is how people see their lives—then the Swiss are the happiest people in the world. If you think happiness is defined by how people* live *their lives through experiences such as smiling and laughing, enjoyment and feeling treated with respect each day—then the happiest people in the world are Latin Americans.*

Well, that's a switcheroo. Smiling and laughing, instead of a ladder.

You might at this point be starting to get suspicious, and wonder about the role of money in all of this. Our pollster continues:

> *If . . . you think happiness is how people see their lives . . . the results are predictable—the wealthiest countries in the world top the list. If you think happiness is not so dependent*

---

1   Gallup supplies the data for the UN report.

on money and is based more on how much people report enjoyment, laughing and smiling—then look no further than Gallup's Global Emotions Report.

Let us look no further, then. The Positive Experience Index in the *Global Emotions Report* ditches the Cantril Ladder and relies on the answers to *five* questions:

- Did you feel well-rested yesterday?
- Were you treated with respect all day yesterday?
- Did you smile or laugh a lot yesterday?
- Did you learn or do something interesting yesterday?
- Did you experience a lot of enjoyment yesterday?

Guess what? The winners in the 2017 *Global Emotions Report* aren't Switzerland and Scandinavia. They're Paraguay, Costa Rica, Panama, the Philippines, and Uzbekistan! The Swiss come in 28th place, with a score of 77 out of 100. (Paraguay's score was 84.) On, *Did you smile or laugh a lot yesterday?* the Swiss did even worse: 50th place out of the 142 countries surveyed. Not even in the top third. And this despite being the wealthiest people in the world (see Question 29).

Of course, you can ask yourself here, as well as with the ladder question, whether Gallup is measuring what it thinks it's measuring. Perhaps what it has found is not a lot of happiness in Paraguay, but a cultural tendency to airbrush the recent past. In which case the *Smug Self-Satisfaction Report* competes here with the *Selective Memory Report.*

So, take your pick. In any case, it's very good to have a number for these things. If anyone asks you how happy the Swiss are, you can tell them, in the first case, to three decimal places; in the second, on a scale 1 to 100. In either case, you ought to satisfy sticklers for precision.

Just hope they don't ask for precision about what the numbers actually mean.

55

What Is Switzerland's Most Offensive Statue?

The old city of Bern, founded in the 12th century, has been a UNESCO Cultural World Heritage Site since 1983. To Henry James, in 1875, it was a puzzling place: he found it

> *homely, ugly, almost grotesque, but full of character. Indeed, I do not know why it should have so much when there are cities which have played twice the part in the world which wear a much less striking costume.*

James goes on to describe the charms of this contradictory character:

> *The houses are gray and uneven, and mostly capped with great pent-house red roofs, surmounted with quaint little knobs and steeples and turrets. They have flower-pots in the windows and red cushions on the sills, on which, toward evening, there are generally planted a pair of solid Bernese elbows. If the elbows belong to a man, he is smoking a big-bowled pipe; if they belong to one of the softer sex, the*

color in her cheeks is generally a fair match to the red in the
cushion.

In 1919 the poet Rainer Maria Rilke noted

How unanimous Bern stands there, every house above its
fretted stone arcades, which draw in even the traffic under
their protection too, so that outside there remain only the
markets and the wonderfully picturesque fountains that make
even the water into a good citizen!

The tourist walks through this charmed city today, enjoy-
ing those wonderfully picturesque fountains, until—horrors!
Here, smack in the middle of the Kornhausplatz, she comes
upon a fountain which is anything but a good citizen. She
has bumped into the *Kindlifresser.*

A *Kindlifresser* is a baby-eater. The ogre towers above the
fountain. His grotesquely wide-open mouth has a baby half
stuffed into it, headfirst, its little legs kicking back in protest.
Three babies are trapped in a bag slung over his shoulder; a
fifth is pressed between his elbow and his torso; a sixth is
floundering from a strap by his right knee; a seventh hides
behind his shoulders; and the eighth, who has broken free, is
escaping around the corner of the pedestal on which the whole
thing stands—with an appropriately gleeful look on his face.

The *Kindlifresser* isn't only offensive if you think it's disgust-
ing to eat babies—especially lots of babies. It's also offensive
because it may well be an anti-Semitic monument. The peaked
hat worn by the giant resembles the one that Jews were required to wear in Bern in the sixteenth century, when the
statue was created. A popular idea at the time had it that Jews

kidnapped and murdered Christian children, and used their blood to make matzos at Passover. This was one of a trio of accusations—the other two being well-poisoning and host desecration—used to justify the persecution of Jews in the Middle Ages.

Of course, the *Kindlifresser* isn't eating matzos—which would definitely make for a less exciting statue. He's cutting right to the chase, and eating the babies directly. So maybe he isn't a Jew—maybe he's a Greek. The Greek titan Cronus ate his own children because he feared that when they grew up they would rise up against him in rebellion. Zeus was one of those children, and was saved at the last minute by his mother, who, after feeding Cronus his other five kids, served him a rock in Zeus's place. Admittedly, it's hard to understand how even a normal father could mistake a rock for one of his children—much less a father who is *eating* them. Old Cronus must have had very bad taste buds and very tough teeth—but maybe that's what titans are like.

Probably one of the best ways to ensure that your children are going to rise up in rebellion against you is to eat them—unsuccessfully. Zeus grew up and *did* rebel, forcing Cronus to vomit up his siblings, who joined him in banishing Dad to Tartarus.

If the *Kindlifresser* is Greek, however, the sculptor didn't get his mythology right.[1] Cronus only had six kids, while the statue shows us eight.

My favorite theory is that the *Kindlifresser* is neither Jewish nor Greek but Swiss—and, not to put too fine a point on it, Bernese. Legend has it that when Berchtold V, Duke of Zähringen, founded Bern in 1191, his older brother went insane with

---

1   Hans Gieng. The statue was made around 1545.

jealousy. This is certainly understandable: after all, if your brother founded a fine city like Bern, destined to be the capital of a beautiful country like Switzerland, you might feel a pang or two of jealousy as well. I'm sure I would. Would you or I do what the duke's older brother did next? Who knows? Insanity is a strange and wonderful state of mind. In any case, older brother rounded up the city's children and—you guessed it—ate them for dinner.

Enough scapegoating. I think the Swiss ought to just own up to this one. Offensive as it may appear, the *Kindlifresser* is one of their own.

56

Where's the Best Place to Spit if I Want My Spittle to Travel Far and Wide?

Not everyone has the infantile urge to conquer the world with their bodily fluids. But the idea that from land-locked Switzerland you can spit into three entirely different bodies of salt water all at the same time is, for some, rather compelling.

If it's compelling for you, you'll definitely want to know about a special place on the Witenwasserenstock—a 3,084-meter-high mountain on the border of Cantons Valais and Uri, about 6 kilometers southeast of the Furka Pass. Head 300 meters to the east of the summit and you'll arrive at a spot known as Point 3,024. Here Canton Ticino joins the party. Politically speaking, it's a triple border point.

More significantly, though, it's a triple watershed. Collect a bunch of saliva in your mouth and spit directly on this point. Your wad of spittle will divide in three: some of it will head north, some south, and some east. The bit heading south will soon find its way onto the Geren Glacier.[1] There it will freeze and, some 1,500 meters and over a decade later (see Question 5), melt and become part of the Gerenwasser. It will flow in this stream for seven kilometers and then join the Rhône. As part of the Rhône your spit will traverse Valais in less than a day, reaching Lake Geneva at the small village of Le Bouveret. Here it will slow down considerably—not as slow as when it was a chunk of Geren Glacier ice, but still slow enough: it takes 11.4 years to cross the lake and arrive in Geneva. There the "divinely cool-hued gush of the Rhône . . . one of the loveliest things in Switzerland" (Henry James) will carry it through the city and westward into France. In France your spittle meanders toward Lyon, then, with more purpose, heads south through Avignon and Arles and out into the Mediterranean, leaving the European continent at a point about 460 kilometers (as the crow flies) from where it started out. It has taken somewhere between twenty and thirty years to reach the sea.

The bit heading north will travel down a few hundred meters of scree and become part of the Witenwasseren Glacier, where it will slowly journey downward for over a decade before melting into the Witenwasserenreuss. At Hospenthal its host will become more pronounceable, dropping the "Witenwasseren" to become the plain old Reuss—the river of Luzern. This Reuss will carry it into Lake Uri at Fluelen.

---

1   This is the most dangerous part of the trip, because here your spittle is most likely to either evaporate or freeze and then sublimate (change directly from ice to gas). Thus it would be practical to spit during a heavy rain, so your saliva gets carried down on the surface of the scree directly to the glacier. If you don't think it's practical for you to be at Point 3,024 on the Witenwasserenstock in the pouring rain, you're quite right. There aren't too many days when it rains up there, either, so you'll probably have to wait a while for ideal conditions—but think of your saliva and its Wanderlust!

From here our spittle will take 3.4 years to reach the city of Luzern and yet again join the Reuss; below Brugg it turns into the Aare, and, near Koblenz, the Rhine. A few weeks later it reaches the North Sea at Hoek van Holland in the Netherlands, 670 kilometers in a direct line from where it started—the entire journey having taken between fifteen and twenty years.

The spittle heading east will miss out on any glaciers on its way to the Rio di Bedretto, from which it will merge into the Ticino River. It will enter Lago Maggiore at Locarno and dawdle for 4 years, finally leaving the lake at Sesto Calende. It will join the Po near Pavia and reach the Adriatic Sea just south of Venice, some 460 kilometers southeast of its starting point. Due to the absence of glacier travel, this trip will be much quicker, taking somewhat less than five years.

Your spittle has traveled for thousands of kilometers through Switzerland, France, Germany, and Italy, and ended up in three entirely different and widely separated bodies of salt water. It has taken from 5 to 25 years for it to complete its various trips, and it has become one of the great European travelers.

I can hear you protesting already: the Adriatic and the Mediterranean aren't actually "entirely different and widely separated," and I guess you have a point. But we can do this even better. Let's hike up to the Lunghin pass, an unprepossessing point on a north-south ridge at only 2,645 meters above sea level and entirely in Canton Graubünden. Despite its relatively low height and the complete absence of glaciers, this is a famous location: the most important divide of the European continent. Spit again! The bit that flows west quickly turns northward and travels via the Julia, then the Albula, then the Hinterrhein, and then the Rhine rivers to the North Sea. But that's not all. Because of a slight shoulder that nudges its way up to the pass from the west, some of that same initially westward-flowing spittle will deviate to the south, hitting the Maira River, then Lake Como, the Adda, the Po, and gushing out into the Adriatic. We've been here before. But now comes the good one: the east. Your spittle flows down into the Lunghinsee, then the Inn and Danube Rivers. It journeys through Austria, Germany, Slovakia, Hungary, Croatia, Serbia, Bulgaria, Romania, Moldova and the Ukraine, finally gushing out into the Black Sea. How's that for "entirely different and widely separated bodies of salt water?"

Such journeys! And it doesn't even have to be your spittle— every time it rains or snows, drops and flakes that fall together toward the pass have to say goodbye to one another as they hit the ground and head off on their long and separate journeys to three different salty seas.

57

What Happens to Swiss Nuclear Waste?

Approximately 60 times per year nuclear fuel and nuclear waste are transported to and from Swiss nuclear power plants, unannounced, by truck or train. The material is sealed in 600-ton cylindrical steel containers, and security is provided by the cantonal police.

If you're a fan of action movies and you're looking for a job, I recommend you try your luck at the place where these steel containers are tested: the German *Bundesamt für Material-forschung und -prüfung,*[1] or, using its acronym, simply, BAM![2] The containers have their own acronym, and are known in the jargon as CASTORs: *Casks for Storage and Transport of Radioactive Material.* Your job is going to be to try to beat these suckers up until they burst.

So let's get started. First of all you'll drop a CASTOR (remember, they weigh 600 tons) from a height of nine meters onto a rigid surface—a *really* rigid surface: a five meter thick steel and concrete foundation topped with a twenty centi-

---

1   Federal Office for Materials Research and Testing.
2   My explanation point—usually abbreviated simply as BAM.

meter steel plate. You'll hoist the CASTOR up inside a massive pylon and then—just let it go. If that goes well, you can move on to the thorn test. This is no ordinary Sleeping Beauty thorn, but a steel prong, 20 centimeters high and 15 across, and you get to drop the CASTOR onto it from a meter in the air. CASTOR still okay? Now drop a half-ton weight onto it from nine meters up. Still good? Then it's time for the helicopter test: a half-scale model CASTOR dangles from a chopper and gets released from 200 meters in the air. Down it comes. BAM! The CASTOR is still doing fine, its seals uncompromised! So it's time for trial by fire: place your CASTOR in the middle of a conflagration, with a temperature of at least 800 degrees Celsius, and leave it there for half an hour. If it's *still* perfectly sealed, you'll try the opposite: place the thing at the bottom of a 200-meter deep pool for an hour— that's a pressure of 200 million pascals.[3] Still no leaks? Okay, time to get extreme: blow up a propane truck next door and see what happens. The truck explodes, the fireball climbs 150 meters into the sky, pieces of the propane tank fly up to 200 meters away, and your 600-ton CASTOR is catapulted seven meters, does a back flip in the air, and is driven a meter deep into the ground. But those seals are *still* holding tight.

So there's only one more thing to do: crash an airplane into it. You don't actually get to use an airplane for this, but you do get to fire a 1,000 kilogram steel projectile at a speed of 300 meters per second (1,080 kilometers per hour) at your cask.

And still the seals all hold.

Now you have an idea of the containers that Swiss nuclear waste travels in. These CASTORs are trained or trucked to an

---

3   Disappointingly, this test is done by computer simulation. All the others are done live and in the flesh.

intermediate storage facility in Würenlingen in Canton Aargau. 34 are currently sitting in the storage hall, and there's room for 166 more. Since Switzerland is phasing out its nuclear power production completely over the next couple of decades, this ought to be sufficient space.

The next step is to find a final resting place for the CASTORs: deep, deep underground. And final means—well, pretty final. Nagra (the National Cooperative for the Disposal of Radioactive Waste) reckons that it will take 200,000 years for the stuff in the CASTORs to decay to safe levels. Three sites have been selected as possibilities for this very-long-term storage, all of them near the German border between Aarau and Schaffhausen, and Nagra will start test-drilling on all three sites in 2019. In 2030, the Federal Council and the Parliament will decide on one of the three. Weak to intermediate-level radioactive waste will start being permanently stored there in 2050; the high-level stuff will have to wait, according to current planning, until a decade later.

2060! This could be called serious long-range planning.

It could also be called a serious *lack* of long-range planning. Switzerland's five nuclear power plants went into operation between 1969 and 1984. We've just seen that, by 2030, Switzerland plans to have figured out what to do with their waste. Elementary arithmetic suggests this plan is being made 61 years too late. Critics suggest it's akin to diving off a high cliff and then checking, as you fall, how deep the water is.

So how deep *is* the water? Well, it's not water, but it is deep. Geological storage for low and medium-level waste will be in a level of rock somewhere between 200 and 800 meters underground. For high-level waste it's between 400 and 900. So the whole shebang will play out between one and three Eiffel towers below the surface of the earth.

This is not nearly as deep as the Gotthard Base Tunnel, at 2,450 meters (see Question 51), but they say it's going to be a pretty stable layer of rock. And if they're not sure how stable it is, I can suggest the people at BAM! They seem to be pretty good at testing that sort of thing.

58

Who Gets Swiss Trains When the Swiss Get Tired of Them?

If you like browsing the classified ads, you might have come upon the following offer under the rubric "Sales of Rolling Stock" in July, 2017:

The Swiss Southeast Railway (SOB) will begin using their new rolling stock for the Voralpen-Express in December, 2019. The former fleet of trains will be offered up on the market. Locomotives of the types Re 446 and Re 456, as well as carriages of the types Revvivo, NPZ-Doublette, and EWI will be for sale.

We will be happy to present the vehicles to interested parties and give advice about taking them on. In the attachment you will find the basic negotiable prices and the catalogue with technical details.

If you are interested, don't hesitate! We're ready to talk!

If you're not interested, maybe the German Federal Railway (DB) will be—in 2011, they bought 15 decommissioned 1970s carriages from the Swiss Federal Railway (SBB) to fill some gaps in their long-distance routes. More exotically, twelve carriages from the Zentralbahn (ZB) found their way to a rail line between Guinea, Togo, and Niger in 2015. They sold for 30,000 francs apiece, rode the rails to Rotterdam, and traveled by ship to west Africa. Both sides enjoyed the negotiations leading up to the sale—the Africans laughed when the Zentralbahn pointed out the advantages of the heating system, and the Swiss found it amusing that the strength of the roof was of primary concern to the Africans—both people and goods would be traveling up there.

In 2016 the SBB set off a minor controversy by selling 25 asbestos-laden carriages to the Czech Republic.[1]

It's unlikely that old train cars will be heading to North Korea anytime soon, but in the good old days before sanctions, the Bern-Lötschberg-Simplon railway (BLS) *donated* several old carriages to the land of Kim Jong-il. Nor were they alone—in 1995 the Zurich Transportation Enterprise (ZVB) provided North Korea with twelve well-used trams. Today they carry passengers to a mausoleum.

Lucky trams. Most decommissioned Swiss trains don't get a second life; they head to the mausoleum themselves. Many are sitting right now on their own death rows—unused tracks in underused train stations. Just *how* many, however, is rather vague. The SBB press office couldn't say, and claimed it would be "difficult to determine."

---

1   According to the SBB, the Czechs promised to remove the asbestos before putting the cars to work.

Sometimes these condemned cars have to wait for years before their execution. Occasionally they become hangouts for local teenagers, either officially because someone buys them for that purpose, or unofficially because they're just there—though this kind of use is strictly forbidden. They are often vandalized. In 2013 arsonists set a fire that destroyed 14 decommissioned carriages in Etzwilen.

Other old cars are luckier. While almost every train you step into in Switzerland feels fresh and spanking new, this is often deceptive—many cars have simply been snazzily refitted. Still, the contrast between Switzerland and neighboring countries, particularly as regards local trains, is striking. It makes you wonder whether the Swiss aren't overdoing it slightly—as with their roads, where the smallest crack in the asphalt tends to be addressed with a complete repaving.

Luckily, there's a watchdog out there. The *Schweizer Eisenbahn-Revue (Swiss Railway Review)* is a monthly magazine with a circulation of 10,000 railway "amateurs"—people who just like trains. And so the decommissioning and destruction of old carriages doesn't go unnoticed.

In 2013 the *Revue* caught the SBB in the act of shredding two separate million-franc locomotives that were only 18 years old. These engines should have had a life span of 40 years. It would have taken 30 just to amortize their price tags. So why were they being reduced to scrap?

Revue chief editor Walter von Andrian was critical. "The trains simply weren't popular with the SBB," he said. The SBB countered that it was merely following its publicly declared strategy of standardizing its fleet.

The moral of the story? If you're a train car, freshen up your appearance as you age. Apply a little make-up. Stay popular.

Otherwise, you might be sent to a mausoleum in North Korea.

Or even worse—to the wrecking claws and the scrap heap.

59

If Switzerland Were a Swimming Pool, How Deep Would It Be?

Since we're going to want a flat bottom for our swimming pool, we first completely level Swiss terrain, filling in all the valleys with the mountains—and leaving the entire country at a uniform elevation of 1,350 meters above sea level (see Question 18). Switzerland's 130 cubic kilometers of lake water is now sitting on top of an elevated Swiss footprint (see Question 35) with an area of 41,285 square kilometers.[1] The water is deeper than the deepest of Olympic swimming pools: to be precise, it's 3.14 meters deep.[2]

But not for long. The mother of all waterfalls will thunder off this Swiss plateau into France, Germany, Liechtenstein and parts of Austria and Italy. Briefly and catastrophically, it will

---

1   For lakes that border other countries, such as Lake Geneva, the figure given includes only the Swiss portion of the Lake.

2   You might recognize 3.14 as a number you know from somewhere else. This is either a mystic discovery of cosmic proportions or a raw coincidence. Since after two decimal places the numbers no longer jive, I have to reluctantly go for the raw coincidence.

make Victoria Falls look like a leaking faucet, and ocean tsunamis look like ripples in a pond.

Unless, of course, we build a border wall to keep the water in. That wall will be 1,935 kilometers long. To make it 3.5 meters high—enough to retain the water but low enough that we can climb out of the pool—we'll need quite a lot of concrete. On the other hand, the Lac de Dix will now be empty, so we can use the stuff from the Dixence dam (See Question 49). Chop it up into blocks and lay them along the border. It's enough to make a wall just under a meter thick.

A meter thick. Hey. We could even lie down on top of the wall to dry off!

Well, not quite. Each Swiss resident would have a 45-centimeter by 45-centimeter square to stand on, and we'd be standing two-deep all along the wall—but hey, we'd fit. And if we made a law that three-fourths of the population always had to be swimming, then the rest of us could lay out our (relatively skinny) towels and enjoy the sun. Or rain. Or snow.

People with vertigo should definitely hug the inside of this wall, though, or head to the southern border. In most places there's a drop of about a kilometer down to the EU. On the other hand, people who like the sun should stick to the north side of the pool—on the border with Italy our wall abuts huge vertical cliffs, some over 3 kilometers high. It's shady and cold down here on the southern frontier.[3]

You might wonder what it would look like if instead of spreading out the lake water we merely melted all the glaciers. It's a bit less deep then, and most adults would be able to stand with

---

3   We didn't really need to build the wall around this part, but we did it anyway—just to show certain politicians how it's done.

their heads and necks out of the water. On the other hand, the water would be really, really cold.

What happens to you if you swim in really cold water was described by Dr. Christopher McStay from the Bellevue Hospital Center in New York, just after treating the survivors of the US Airways flight that made an emergency landing in the Hudson River in January, 2009.

> *When you first go into extremely cold water there is this weird response called a cold shock response. People start to hyperventilate immediately. For one to three minutes you breathe very fast and deep, uncontrollably . . . Once that response goes away, you're fine . . . for a while.*
>
> *Generally, a person can survive in 5-degree C water for 10, 15 or 20 minutes before the muscles get weak and you lose coordination and strength—which happens because the blood moves away from the extremities and toward the center, or core, of the body.*

If we've just melted the glaciers, our water's going to be even colder than the Hudson River in midwinter. This does not sound pleasant.

Our wall, of course, could now be lower, so we could make it twice as wide—giving each of us a spot (almost) for a meter-long towel.

None of this sounds like much fun. But thinking about it sure makes you glad that Switzerland has over 1,500 lakes—and 1,400 glaciers—all of which are working hard and doing a pretty good job of keeping the rest of the country dry.

60

If Switzerland Were Placed under a Dome, Would it Survive?

The orthodox view is stated by Dieter Freiburghaus, Professor for Europe at the University of Lausanne:

> Whoever seriously talks about an independent Switzerland is either promoting folklore or is miserably ignorant of the tight web of international relations that makes this country possible. Switzerland would hardly survive for more than a few weeks if it truly closed its borders.

Professor Freiburghaus is surely correct: the Switzerland we know would not survive a dome. But what about the Swiss people?

Switzerland has the smallest amount of utilized agricultural land per inhabitant of any European country besides the Netherlands. If this land were evenly divided, every resident would receive a plot with an area of about 1,225 square meters (35 meters on each side). For comparison, a Spaniard gets a plot four times as large.[1]

It gets worse for the Swiss, however, because 70 percent of this utilized agricultural land grows grass, not crops! The portion of the 1,225 square-meter Swiss plot growing grain, vegetables, and fruit consists of a mere 370 square meters—a square with sides only 19 meters long.

In addition to this land, which is mostly on the Swiss plateau and relatively flat by Swiss standards, the Swiss each get a bonus: a mostly steep, somewhat rocky plot, covered with snow most of the year, but in the summer sprinkled with wildflowers and covered with luscious grass—625 square meters of alp, which is a square 25 meters on each side.

If we picture the Swiss sitting on their mostly grassy 35 meter squares of land, with, for the sake of our fiction, a steeper and much higher 25 meter square of alp attached, we have to picture some company as well. Among every five of these combined plots roams a cow and a pig, and everybody has his or her own chicken. A few people even have two chickens. One in every hundred plots has a goat on it, and one in twenty-four a sheep. The majority of these animals move from the larger plot to the smaller for a couple of months in the summer.

A few of these cows, pigs, sheep, chickens and goats eat fodder imported from other countries. But those fed only on the products of Swiss soil are still able to provide 75 percent of the calories the Swiss get from dairy, meat and eggs. Meanwhile their cultivated land produces 50 percent of their plant-based calories. Combining the two, Switzerland produces 60 percent of the number of calories it eats. This compares favorably with Japan (40 percent) and Norway (50 percent),

---

1   Italians, surprisingly, get less than double what the Swiss do, and—surprise again—Denmark does practically as well as Spain.

but poorly with most other European countries, which produce more calories than they consume.

What makes the scenario rosier is that the Swiss currently eat (or waste) a lot of calories every day: over 3,000 of them. If the dome came down and all else remained the same, 60 percent would still give every Swiss person some 1,800 calories to survive on. This is barely enough—if all they did was lie in bed all day. But they can't all lie in bed all day, because then no one would be working the fields, and pretty soon they'd all have *zero* calories.

So there's no way around it: we need to make more calories available.

And thereby hangs a tale.

On the 15th of November, 1940, with the Swiss soon to be surrounded by hostile powers, a Swiss bureaucrat named Friedrich Traugott Wahlen gave a naughty speech. Naughty because Wahlen, who worked at the Federal Office of Wartime Nutrition, gave the speech without permission from his superiors. It delineated what would come to be called *Plan Wahlen*—a strategy he had worked out on his own some years before. The Swiss government was—at least at first—dead against this plan. It resonated with the Swiss people, however.

Plan Wahlen called for Switzerland to be turned, as far as possible, into a garden. At the time Wahlen gave his speech, 183,000 hectares of Swiss land was dedicated to growing crops. Wahlen wanted to triple this. Animal agriculture was to be cut back, since, as any vegan will tell you, it's a very inefficient way of producing nutrients. Meadows were to be tilled and turned to cultivated land, while new gardens were to be established everywhere—on rooftops, in stray lots, on lawns and in parks. The *Anbauschlacht*—the Food-Growing

Battle—became a way for the Swiss to express their pride and independent spirit during a terrible war.

Plan Wahlen was effective. It never quite got up to the 500,000 hectares Wahlen had envisaged, but it doubled the amount of large-scale cultivated land. In addition, it saw some 20,000 hectares of small gardens spring up, tended by ordinary citizens. Between 1939 and 1945, the grain harvest doubled, the potato harvest tripled, and the vegetable harvest quadrupled. According to some estimates, Switzerland went from being 52 percent self-sufficient to almost 80 percent.

At the same time, the average number of calories eaten by the Swiss took a hit, dropping from 3,200 to 2,200 per day. But this was enough. No one was starving. And potatoes, vegetables and fruit never had to be rationed.

Clearly, if the dome were to descend today, Switzerland would need a new *Plan Wahlen*. The borders were never completely sealed during World War II; trade, in a reduced form, continued. The dome and today's larger population would provide an even greater challenge than the war.

The new *Plan Wahlen* would involve changing over completely to organic agriculture, as neither chemical fertilizers nor the petrochemicals to make them could be imported.[2] It would involve oxen replacing tractors, and scythes, rakes and wagons replacing mowing machines and hay trucks. Essentially, it would involve becoming Amish—and this is entirely appropriate, as the Amish came from Switzerland.[3]

Organic agriculture, especially without machinery, is very labor-intensive. However, contrary to popular opinion, it represents a *more* efficient use of *land*. And this fits in with our

---

2   12 percent of Swiss farms are already organic.
3   Jakob Ammann was born in Erlenbach.

dome very nicely, for we have little land, but *lots* of unemployed people. Think of all those bankers, hoteliers, arms manufacturers, diplomats, industrialists, and and and, who no longer have the raw materials, communications or clients to continue with their businesses. That's a lot of neophyte organic farmers.

Our domed-in Swiss will need some energy in other forms than food calories. Switzerland keeps four and a half months of strategic oil reserves.[4] This could be stretched, to be sure, but would eventually run out. Stores of enriched uranium would run out as well.

Luckily, over 50 percent of Switzerland's electricity is provided by hydropower (see Question 41). So when the uranium reserves run out, we'll still have half the electricity we do today. Losing half your electricity is a big hit—but on the other hand, there's all that industry that isn't running anymore. Keeping the hydropower plants operating without machinery driven by fossil fuels will be a challenge, but not an insuperable one. We can probably replace much of that machinery with electrically-driven analogues—raw materials for which might come from the over 6 million trucks, cars and motorcycles, the over 3,000 airplanes, and the almost 100,000 power boats which will no longer be good for much else.

Keeping warm in winter will be a challenge. 10 percent of Switzerland's heating is done with wood, and there's capacity to double that before it gets unsustainable—again, it would be labor-intensive without fossil fuel, but again, we've got labor. 20 percent of heating is currently provided by heat pumps, which run on electricity. That's 40 percent of our heating needs

---

4   The US, by contrast, has 35 days worth.

covered. New living arrangements, at least in winter, would be necessary to stay warm. But with a bit of huddling together, it could be done.

To stay warm we'll need more than huddling and heat pumps—we need clothing. There is so much more of this in 21st-century closets and shops than anybody conceivably has need for, that we will surely survive on it for some time. And make a very fashionable set of organic gardeners, to boot. After this all wears out we'll have to go back to the old ways, using Swiss wool, flax and hemp to make our own. And wear our outfits, as in the old days, for months at a time.

Our collective health will suffer. Many people will die of illnesses that could be cured or prevented today. There won't be enough energy or equipment or medications to keep hospitals running at anything like their current standards, so the population will likely decline—with the advantage that the survivors will have more calories to live on.

So far we've been assuming a benevolent dome in one important respect, and it has allowed us to skip over the most essential factors for survival: water and air. Our dome has been permeable to the climate, and hasn't affected the weather systems, oxygen exchange, or temperatures. In addition, it has allowed rivers to carry water across the borders into other lands, and evaporated water to escape into the atmosphere.

If our dome were not permeable to the weather and the rivers, things would look quite different. With no influx and outflow of water, Switzerland would rather quickly dry up. Although lakes would form or increase in size at the former exit points of the major rivers, especially around Basel, Geneva, Martina and Locarno, the evaporation from them wouldn't make up for the 60 billion cubic meters that currently fly in annually from the oceans, seas, and Eurasian continent, or the 13 billion that enter in streams and rivers. Switzerland might turn into a strange contradiction: a desert punctuated with large lakes and swamps. Our gardens wouldn't grow, temperatures would run haywire, and the oxygen/CO_2 balance would cease to be life-supporting.

The most extensive experiment with life in a vivarium, the Biosphere 2 project in Oracle, Arizona in the early 1990s, kept its team of eight human beings alive in a completely closed system[5] for two years, but this closed system—of only 3.14 hectares—was intricately planned. Inside its several domes were to be found a mini-rain forest, a mini-ocean, a mangrove wetlands, a fog desert, and solar heating and cooling systems. Unless whoever dropped the dome on Switzerland was an awesome engineer and provided some unparalleled infrastructure along with it, a non-permeable dome would definitely see our doom.

So let's hope the dome was just a metaphor for economic and political isolation from the countries outside Swiss borders, and not from the rest of the natural world. We need nature far more than international trade.

---

5   Well, almost. There were a couple of interventions.

61

How Often are the Clocks in Swiss Train Stations Wrong?

One hundred percent of the time.

If you've ever been in a Swiss train station you've surely noticed a subtly intriguing phenomenon. The strangely shaped red second-hand of the railway clock reaches the top of the dial and conspicuously pauses; time seems to stand still; you wait, out of breath, as the clock seems to be waiting; and then suddenly: *thunk*—release—the black minute-hand jumps to the next mark on the dial, and the second-hand takes up its regular journey around the clock face.

If you think about it, this has to mean that either the minute-hand or the second-hand is off. Either the minute-hand has waited too long to lunge, or the second-hand has got to the top of the dial too early, and therefore has to wait.

Train schedules are calibrated in minutes, not seconds, so you might guess that the minute-hand is the sacred one on this clock. And you'd be right. It's the red hand that goes too fast, completing its circuit in 58.5 seconds rather than the 60 that it ought to take. It waits for 1.5 seconds at the top.

This means, in turn, that the clock is only ever right at the exact instant when the minute hand jumps and the second hand begins to move again. At every other instant, the clock is running slightly fast.

The clock thus only reads the right time once a minute, on the minute. It's correct at 9:11:00, and then at 9:12:00, and then 9:13:00, and so on. But it's only correct *exactly* at that instant, and that instant doesn't last for any time. It's not right from 9:12:00 to 9:12:01, because during that one-second interval the second hand has been moving too fast. It's not even right from 9:12:00.0 to 9:12:00.1, because even in that one-tenth of a second interval the second hand has moved too fast. You can play this game *ad infinitum*—with the conclusion that the instant 9:12:00.000 . . . , with an infinite number of zeros trailing after it, has no duration. It's an exact time, not an interval. It's a time, yes, but it *takes up no time.*

The Swiss train station clock may be correct once every minute, but the length of time that it *remains* correct at that exact instant is zero. So the clock isn't always wrong, and yet it's wrong 100 percent of the time!

Now Switzerland is world famous for its clocks and watches, and one of the most important places in the world for a timepiece is a train station.[1] And the Swiss clearly have the means

---

1   In fact, train stations are the reason for the way we measure time today. Before trains, each village had its own local time, with noon falling at the moment when the sun was highest in the sky. Trains needed synchronized time, however, if they were to perform according to schedule: noon in Zurich had to be the same as noon in Basel. With the invention of time zones, times were adjusted—falsified, you could say—so that local noon, in general, no longer corresponded to noon on the clock.

to make a railway clock that's right *all the time*. So why do they use one that's almost always wrong?

The Swiss station clock was designed in 1944 by Hans Hilfiker, an SBB employee, and it has been a phenomenal success. Not only have countries all over Europe adopted it for their own train stations; it has found its way into the Museum of Modern Art in New York and the Design Museum in London. Apple, with its own fetish for design, reportedly spent over 20 million dollars for the right to use it on the iOS 6 iPhones and iPads—after first attempting to swipe it for free.

The first version of Hilfiker's clock looked a little different from the one we see today: it was missing the second-hand. Since it's the minute-hand and not the second-hand that tells station masters, conductors and train drivers when a train can leave the station, a second-hand was not so vital. The important thing was that all the clocks in the station read the same time. Hilfiker's clocks were so constructed that the minute hands on all of them were controlled by a single master clock, which told them when to take the plunge from one mark on the dial to the next.

In 1947, Hilfiker added the second-hand to his clock. Its unusual shape recalls the signaling disk waved by a conductor or station master as a sign to the driver to depart. But this hand was an afterthought. Unlike on most watches, in which the movement of the minute-hand depends on the movement of the second-hand, on Hilfiker's clock it was the opposite— the minute-hands were already sorted and connected. The second-hand was just tacked on.

If you have a second-hand that goes even slightly too fast or too slowly and just keeps going all the time, eventually it will wind up completely out of synch with the lunges of the minute hand. So Hilfiker came up with a brilliant solution: have the second-hands go purposefully slightly too fast, but let them be blocked at the top of the dial and only released with the already synchronized movements of the minute hands. The blockage and release happened through a mechanical device that physically stopped the second hand at the top until released by the minute hand's jump.

The technology has long existed, of course, that obviates the need for such a device; the hands today *could* be perfectly aligned. But why mess with a good thing? If you've made it into MOMA and the Design Museum, if Apple buys your rights for millions, if commuters have developed a real affection for you—isn't beauty more important than accuracy?

I like it how it is. There's something profoundly pleasing in that coordinated *pause . . . jump* ritual—some might even say, something mildly erotic. And of course it's ironically satisfying to know that the clocks of the world's most punctual and best-used railway system so very seldom tell the truth.[2]

---

2   What is truth? I've been assuming in this answer that the "right" time is the conventional one we human beings have agreed on. But not only is this time a lie due to the artificial time zones mentioned in the last footnote—even the idea of a 24-hour day is false. No days (periods starting when the sun is highest in the sky and lasting until the next time it's at its peak) last that long. 24 hours is a "mean solar day"—a fabrication we have defined by averaging the lengths of real days.

Going one step farther, there are no numbers in nature—numbers are tools we use to measure things. It is never 12 o'clock in the universe—12 o'clock is rather a reading on a human measuring device. Seeing time in terms of numbers is putting the cart before the horse—yet it's a habit very hard to break away from. For a brilliant discussion of the falseness of measured time, see Jay Griffiths' outrageous book, *Pip, Pip*.

62

How Much Money Would the Ice In Swiss Glaciers Be Worth If It Were Chopped Into Ice Cubes and Sold?

There are still about 54 billion cubic meters of ice in Swiss glaciers (down from 130 billion in 1850). This makes about 49 trillion kilograms of ice, or about one trillion 10-pound bags. A 10-pound bag of ice sells for between one and three dollars at a typical US gas station, so calling it two bucks we end up with roughly 20 trillion dollars. This is more than the US GDP, which was 18.6 trillion in 2016.[1]

Enough ice to outperform the US economy—that's a lot of ice! Here's another way to look at it. Let's say you were to build a square tower of ice. You're simply going to pile blocks of ice one on top of the other. Each block is a cube 50 centimeters

---

1   The GDP is the total value of everything produced in the country in a year.

on each side. By the time you've piled up four of them, you've reached the height of your average NBA basketball player. By the time you've got 280 of them sorted, you've passed the Jet d'Eau in Geneva at its maximum. 1,656 of them have got you higher than the world's tallest building, the Burj Khalifa in Dubai. But you keep on going, until you run out of ice. How high would this tower be if you were to use all the ice in Swiss glaciers today? Would it reach the clouds? The stratosphere? Outer space? The Moon?

None of all that. This tower would reach past the sun.[2]

There's a big problem with our entrepreneurial scheme to outdo the US economy, however. Ice costs about two bucks a bag at a gas station *now*. If we flooded the market with Swiss glacier ice, the price per bag would fall dramatically.

Leslie Stephen (see Question 32) tried to explain the allure that the Alpine wilderness held for citified Victorian gentlemen by remarking that "Ice is a nuisance in Greenland, and an inestimable luxury at Calcutta." If we flooded the US market with glacier ice, those gas station bags would go from being an inestimable luxury—or at least a convenience worth paying two bucks for—to an inestimable nuisance. There are approximately 170,000 gas stations in the US today, and if we divided the glacier ice among them they would each get close to 6 million bags—meaning that each gas station would be buried in a rectangular mound of ice with a base the size of a football field and a height of 50 meters.[3] This would truly be an inestimable nuisance. No one would give a fig for a bag of ice anymore. In fact, drivers would pay to get *rid* of

---

2   There might be some technical difficulties with melting here, but let's ignore them.
3   Either kind of football field. Take your pick—we're not being that exact here.

them, so they could fill up their gas tanks again and be able to drive.

But how to get rid of them? Let's say we decided to dig a hole and carted all the bags of ice away from the buried gas stations to the hole. The hole is the size of a football field. How deep would we have to dig it?

Unfortunately, we'd have to dig it about 8,500 kilometers deep. Our hole goes all the way down to the center of the earth, and then some. And I seem to remember that it's terribly hot down there.[4]

Well, at least that would get rid of the ice. But stay away from that steaming football field!

Another problem with our scheme has to do with false advertising. We would surely want to market our ice as the purest imaginable, coming as it does from the pristine heights of the Swiss Alps. Depressingly, however, our ice is anything but pristine. Sure, we can filter out the hundreds of corpses (see Question 5) and tons of gravel currently locked into our product, but we'd have to try to hush up a disturbing 2009 study by Christian Bogdal of the Swiss Institute for Chemical and Bio-engineering. Bogdal was trying to explain why pollution from things like dioxins, PCBs, organochlorine pesticides and synthetic musk fragrances has been *increasing* in lakes and rivers since the late 1990s, even though regulations have long since *reduced* their use. His conclusion? Swiss glaciers are polluted. They have been acting for decades as a storehouse for

---

4   Like 6000 degrees Celsius, or 10800 Fahrenheit—about as hot as the surface of the sun. Damn, this keeps happening to us.

airborne pollutants, and now, as they rapidly melt due to global warming, they are setting their stores free and releasing contamination collected in the 1960s, '70s, and '80s.

Our ice is tainted. However, perhaps we can grease a few palms and keep these results under wraps. People believe what they want to believe, and surely no one wants to think of the Swiss Alps as a contaminated area.

The idea of selling glacier ice might sound absurd—but it isn't new. In fact, it has been done quite successfully. In 1865 a man named Marcel Robatel was granted rights to the Trient Glacier in Valais. He employed thirty men to blast apart the glacier's tongue with TNT, then move the chunks of ice with long poles onto a kind of water slide, on which they traveled down to Martigny. From there, once weekly, a train took the harvest to Paris. Café customers could now be served cold lemonade, and butchers were happy that their meat stayed fresh. The Rhône Glacier was also harvested for a time, supplying ice to breweries in Luzern. The Grindelwald glaciers were mined as well. When industrial methods for producing ice became cost-effective towards the turn of the 20th century, the glacier ice businesses—which had flourished for several decades—went bankrupt, and the glaciers were left in peace. So our plan isn't actually crazy—it just comes a couple of centuries too late.

Not as *too late*, however, as if we'd had it a few decades from now. At least today the ice—polluted though it is—is there to harvest. If we really want to do it, though, we'd better hurry up. Glaciologist Matthias Huss of the Federal Institute of Technology says "There's no rescuing the Swiss glaciers. Any slowdown in global warming will come too late." Even with the greatest conceivable reduction in greenhouse gases, he says, 80 to 90 percent of the ice will be gone by 2100. "I only hope," say Samuel Nussbaumer of the University of Zurich, "that we will be able to preserve at least a few small pieces of the very highest glaciers."

It looks as if, by 2100, ice will have become an inestimable luxury in the Swiss Alps.

63

Can Swiss Currency Be Counterfeited?

In 2016 authorities confiscated over 8,000 counterfeit bills and coins with a total value—or non-value—of almost 400,000 francs. Twelve people were convicted of counterfeiting, and 95 of circulating false money.

The problem with all of these counterfeits, though, is that they weren't any good. Over 1,000 of the false notes were color photocopies, and the rest were made with ink-jet printers. And a photocopier and an ink-jet printer just aren't up to this job.

Swiss notes are equipped with a vast array of security features, from holograms to embossings to perforations—yes, tiny holes in the paper, in the shape of a number or a cross.[1] Some features are visible only in ultraviolet or infrared light. The newest bills are designed to transfer traces of color onto white paper when rubbed.

A glossy strip runs across the bottom of the new 50-franc note. It contains, in shiny silver, a map of Switzerland, a

---

1   Hold one up to a light and you'll see.

drawing of the Alps, the names of the main four-thousand-meter peaks in Switzerland, and the number 50. Tilt the note backwards, and the outlines of Switzerland and the Alps appear in rainbow colors, while little shining Swiss crosses become visible inside the number 50. Tilt the note from left to right: red and green numbers appear on four different lines. As you tilt further, the numbers move across the note in opposite directions.

Another security feature is the use of micro-lettering. Texts in tiny, tiny writing—visible only with a powerful magnifying glass—are hidden at various points on the note in four different languages. Two of those texts on the 8th series 200-franc note are buried in the hair of the man looking out at us with weary eyes from the brownish-yellow background. That man is C.F. Ramuz, and the texts read:

Charles Ferdinand Ramuz, one of the greatest storytellers of our time, is considered the founder of modern literature in French Switzerland. His work depicts people in tragic conflict with the powers of nature. His finely wrought language employs modes of expression borrowed from both painting and film.

This microtext fails to mention that one of Ramuz's best-loved works—as we have already seen (Question 46)—is a semi-historical novel about a very successful counterfeiter.

So assuming we want to counterfeit Swiss money *well*—how hard *is* it? I asked Mark Turnage, the CEO of Dark Owl Security Services. Here's what he said:

Any object made by one man can within reason be "remade" by another. With enough resources and technology anything can be recreated—counterfeited. However, the reality is that there aren't unlimited resources, and some things are much, much harder to counterfeit than others. The Swiss currency would be in that category. The range and number of security features found in the notes, as well as the overall design, certainly puts the Swiss currency at the very top of the list of the world's most secure and difficult-to-counterfeit notes. Like many other things Swiss, they are immaculately designed, extremely well produced, and beautiful to the eye. Counterfeiters beware.

On the other side of the fence stands Hans-Jürgen Kuhl—a graphic designer turned counterfeiter who was undone in 2006 when a forklift at a dump in Cologne poked through a garbage bag and revealed shredded misprints of 100-dollar bills—and, unhappily for Kuhl, an invoice with his name and address on it. Kuhl's 16.5 million false dollars were, according to the German Federal Criminal Police Office, "terrifyingly perfect." The judge who condemned him to six years imprisonment simultaneously praised him as an "extraordinary graphic artist."

Asked by the Swiss online news service *Watson* if the new Swiss notes are secure, Kuhl replied

Certainly not. All of the safety features can be counterfeited nowadays. It's just a question of effort. The silver hologram on the new notes is only about 1.5 centimeters wide—that's ridiculous. It makes it easy for counterfeiters.

But Kuhl doesn't think false francs are worth the bother.

The market is simply too small—no one worth his salt would want to do it. Why should they? With the same expenditure

*of effort you can make dollars or euros, which you can cir-
culate in many more countries.*

So he advises taking the middle way:

*First you need a good photocopier, and they aren't cheap—
at least 10,000 francs. You can easily get a suitable natural
paper, one that won't glow blue under a UV lamp. If you
want to get rid of a banknote in a bar at night, that's all you
need.*

Yet another middle way doesn't involve printing anything at
all, but rather goes directly to the source. Swiss banknotes are
printed by the company Orell-Füssli in Zurich. In the summer
of 2012, 1,800 almost finished 1,000-franc notes (see Question
20) disappeared from the press. Two men were later arrested
at a currency exchange in London trying to cash in 37 of the
incomplete notes—which were noticed because they had no se-
rial numbers. Orell Füssli promised to "painstakingly review
its security measures in detail."

As well they might. For, according to Edwin Schmidheiny
of Accent Brand Consultants, Swiss bills are more than a store
of value. "As a well-known financial center, our banknotes are
an excellent opportunity to demonstrate our global presence,
and are an expression of our pride." As the publication *MK
Marketing & Kommunikation* puts it, banknotes are a country's
calling card.

Are all the expensive Swiss security features worth it? Perhaps not to prevent counterfeits: a Kuhl can outwit them, and
an amateur would be outwitted by much less. But they sure do
make a splash for the Swiss brand on the international stage—
and that, perhaps, is their ultimate purpose.

64

Do You Need a PhD to Vote in Swiss Elections?

WARNING: Swiss elections are complex. Some might even say, confusing. Some might even say, if you value your sanity, don't go there.

If you understand the next several paragraphs, my hat is off to you. If you don't, I will have made my point. They are intended to enlighten you as to the level and kind of complexity involved in Swiss voting, rather than make you a connoisseur.

I have just cast my vote in the 2018 election for the parliament (*Grossrat*) of Canton Bern. There are 160 seats up for grabs. 2,110 candidates are running on a total of 146 lists with 34 *apparentments*.

Luckily, I only have to worry about my district—the Oberland. Here there are only 224 candidates running, on 14 lists, with 4 *apparentments* and 4 *sub-apparentments*, and I only have to vote for 16 candidates—the number of Oberland parliamentarians. Each of 8 parties has made a list with suggested candidates; some parties have made two lists; one party has made three lists. Some of the 224 separate candidates are actually the same person, however, who appears twice on the same list. This might sound highly illegal, but in Switzerland no one bats an eye.

I can choose a list, or I can make my own. I can choose a list and cross out some people and write in people from another list—this is called making *panaché*, which is a drink that combines beer and lemonade. I can cross out one candidate on a list and write in another candidate's name for the second time—this is called doubling. I can cross out a candidate and leave the space blank, which means I'm giving that vote to the *party* who made the list but not to any particular *candidate*—this is called striking.

When all the votes are in, the parliamentary seats will be divided first among the parties or *apparentments*, and in a second step among the candidates. In order to divide the seats among the parties or *apparentments*, the Swiss Federal Statistical Institute has invented a creature known as the "fictional voter." The number of fictional voters for a given party is the number of votes for that party divided by the average number of valid votes per voter—to remember that quickly, just think: votes over votes per voter. Try not to understand it, because you might lose your mind. Once the number of fictional voters per party is known, it is compared to the total number of fictional voters to determine each party's or *apparentment's* relative strength. The seats in parliament are then divided up according to the Hagenbach-Bishchoff system.

The Hagenbach-Bischoff system was named after the Swiss physicist Eduard Hagenbach-Bischoff (b. 1833). The system is a variant of the D'Hondt method, which itself uses the Hare quota. The Hagenbach-Bishchoff system has the advantage of allocating the greatest number of seats before the implementation of the D'Hondt method.

* * *

If this all sounds like Greek to you, it's merely because you never got that PhD. Actually, to tell the truth, none of my PhD friends understands it either. I know one post-doc who claims to get it, but he's a generally pompous person, and I'm not sure whether to believe him or not.

Examples always help, though. In the 2007 National Council election in Canton Jura, in which only two seats were up for grabs, the parties received the following percentage of the fictional votes:

SP: 36.9%
CVP: 25%
SVP: 13.7%
FDP: 13.4%

The two seats, naturally, went to the SP and the SVP. Before you cry foul, let me inform you that the SVP and the FDP had formed an *apparentment*. Thus you see that *apparentment* is not a typo for apartment, but is actually a technical term for a political move that, if I were from the CVP, I would call cheating; if I were from the SVP, I would call clever positioning; and if I were from the FDP, I'd say, I think we just got used.

Luckily, when I cast my vote, I didn't have to think of any of this. Being a smart voter (even without a PhD) I went to www .smartvote.ch. I answered 60 questions concerning issues relevant to the coming cantonal election, and weighted them according to how important they were to me. smartvote then told me which candidates agree with me the most. I decided to double up (vote twice for) the candidates with views closest to mine. This allowed me to have more influence on the prospects of a smaller number of candidates than if I had given my 16 votes to 16 different people.

In the 2015 national election almost 500,000 of the 2,500,000 Swiss who voted used smartvote to help them decide what to do. This of course gives the platform an enormous influence. And suggests that the most powerful actor in Swiss elections might not be a politician—it might be an equation. Here's the formula that smartvote uses to calculate the closeness of candidates' views to one's own:

$$dist(v,c) = \sqrt{\sum_{i=1}^{n} (v_i - c_i)^2}$$

Since I don't have a PhD in mathematics, this is also Greek to me. I even think I spy a real Greek letter there. But I'm grateful to this mysterious collection of symbols nonetheless. It makes the prospect of voting in Switzerland less overwhelming. PhD or no, I can participate in Switzerland's legendary (and legendarily complex) democracy.

All joking aside—and none of the above is untrue—there is a method to this madness. According to the group *Democracy Building*

> *[The] interesting peculiarities in Switzerland's election system refine a basically* proportional *election system in a unique way so that it features the essential positive aspects of the* majority *election system while avoiding its fundamental drawbacks.*

In a proportional system, as in Germany, residents of a given district vote to fill *several* seats in the parliament. These several seats are divided among several parties, according to the fraction of the vote that they each receive. Parties that receive few votes get few seats, and parties that get many votes get many seats. The parties determine who fills their seats by making a list of their candidates in order of preference. If a party wins two seats, the top two candidates on the list get them. If it wins three seats, the top three on the list get them. And so on.

In a majority system, as in the US, voters in a given district vote to fill a *single* seat in parliament. The candidate who gets the most votes is the only one who wins. His party, of course, has won as well, and is the only one to represent the district. Parties besides the winning one get no representation at all. Such a set-up tends automatically to lead to a two-party system, since only the top two parties have a realistic chance of getting enough votes to win seats.

Switzerland combines these systems. Districts vote for several seats, which are divvied up proportionally among several parties, but voters choose which individual candidates will fill those parties' seats. As the platform *Global Advocacy* notes,

> *Although a Swiss party still controls whether or not a candidate gets listed, it cannot determine a candidate's chances of election through rank on the list. Once candidates are listed, they are on their own and must try to get a maximum number of voters to write them in twice, and a minimum to cross them out.*

One of the consequences of this mix is the increased influence of interest groups.

Although this system seems to give great power to the electorate, it also increases the influence of interest groups. These groups inform their members about the candidates who favor their interests and for whom two votes should be cast, as well as about candidates who should be crossed out because they do not favor the group's interests. A teachers' group, for example, will inform its members which candidates are sympathetic to teachers' needs and which are not.

So if you're ever looking to start a democracy, make sure to look beyond the traditional two types, and consider Switzerland's compromise between majority and proportional systems. At times it seems unimaginably complex, but when it comes right down to it, there may be a certain advantage to being forced to *think*—and think hard—before you cast your ballot.

65

If You Made a Snowman With All the Snow That Falls on Switzerland in a Year, How Tall Would it Be?

Every year about 200 cubic kilometers of fluffy snow falls on Switzerland. This is the equivalent of a cube almost six kilometers on each side.

Snow gets denser as soon as more snow falls on top of it, however, so the volume of the same amount of snow is always changing. Once it settles, our 200 cubic kilometers is going to give us about 80 cubic kilometers of the packable, snowman-building stuff. If we make the snowman in the traditional way, with three huge snowballs of decreasing size atop one another, each one half the volume of the one below it, we'll get a snowman 10.8 kilometers high.

On a good day, this snowman extends from the Swiss plateau to the stratosphere.[1]

There are a couple of problems with this snowman. First of all, it won't really be this high, because its immense weight will compress the snow much more than in a normal snowpack. But the snow will only get compressed vertically, so instead of three round balls we'll end up with three oblongs. Worse than that, the compression will be more in the middle of the balls, where more snow is piled up, than on the sides— so instead of having ellipses we might end up with three kidney-shaped snowmasses nestled on top of one another. This is not very aesthetically pleasing.

Second, we have to find a place to put the thing. Assuming we want to keep it in Switzerland, we'll need to look for a fairly large uninhabited area, with at least a 3-kilometer radius—so when the bottom ball smushes down it won't destroy any houses.

We'll also want to maintain the hydrologic balance in Europe as best we can. This snowman is going to be an ecological catastrophe—it's robbed one-third of Switzerland's annual precipitation—but we can at least try to limit the damage. To do this we'll need to figure out where Switzerland's water exits the country, and try to place the snowman strategically so that when it eventually melts that balance will be maintained.

Okay, I've looked it up. Water leaves Switzerland primarily in the Rhine (65%), Rhône (24%) and Ticino (7%) rivers. This tells us—because we've all been reading this book attentively, and remember Question 56—this tells us exactly where to put the snowman.

---

1   On a good day, because the altitude of the stratosphere varies.

Yes! You're right! We obviously need to place it at Point 3,024 on the east ridge of the Witenwasserenstock—the triple watershed that will distribute our snow among exactly these three rivers.

Happily, this point also fulfills our other criterion—no dwellings within a three-kilometer radius. Well, almost. I see two Ticinese alphuts that will have to go, and the Swiss Alpine Club won't be too happy about the fate of its Rotondo hut—but hey, if some place has to be destroyed by three gigantic balls piled up on one another, what better name for it than Rotondo?

Well, that's about it. There are a bunch of peaks that will stick up into the bottom snowball and hold it steady, and since we're already up at 3,000 meters, that will compensate for some of the compression, and on good days our snowman might still reach the stratosphere. The skyline of Switzerland is looking a bit different now, and there may be some extremely large avalanches to look forward to in the future—if our man ever tips over. On the other hand, Switzerland now boasts the highest mountain in the world, people will have to learn to say Witenwasserenstock without stumbling on its syllables, and climbers from all over will vie to be the first to ascend it; then the first to ascend it without oxygen; then the first to ascend it solo; then the first to ski down it (this could be tough); then the fastest to get to the top; then the oldest to ascend it—and all the other records that Mount Everest has incited up to now and which have suddenly lost much of their value as braggadocio.

Nicest of all, however, instead of carrying a flag to plant on the summit, these climbers will be carrying other things— objects a bit friendlier and less aggressive: some raisins, a carrot, and a black bowler hat.

66

What Is Switzerland?

Switzerland is a tiny country, less than 350 kilometers long, 220 wide and 5 high, folded up into mountains that double its surface area. Its 1,500 lakes and 1,400 glaciers form the reservoir of Europe. Its high mountains are home to some 40 wolves, 170 lynx, 330 golden eagles and a bear or two, who face off against a human population of 8.5 million. These humans have reshaped much of the land, constructing the world's tallest dam, its longest tunnel, its largest and most intense scientific laboratory, and a quadrillion dollars' worth of other buildings. They have created the world's most intricate and responsive democracy, by means of which they rule over their rulers. They travel on the world's most punctual and intensively used railway network and have the world's most satisfying sex; their children sport in fountains before their rulers' palace, while, unsuspected to them, gnomic figures in vaults beneath their little feet count and care for untold bars of gold. On hot summer days in the medieval cities a half-naked populace jumps from high bridges into wide green rivers of cool glacial water. Government ministers ride on public busses, suicide is accepted and assisted, prostitution is legal, taxed and earns social benefits, heroin is free, trespassing is encouraged, the unemployed go on vacation, criminals are rarely imprisoned, and the dignity of rodents is protected by federal laws.

This country has a dark side. African child labor makes its chocolate; dictators deposit stolen millions in its banks; its tunnels were built under conditions little removed from slavery; mass shootings and other gun deaths rank far above the norm; minarets have been outlawed; arms exports are among the world's highest; disappearing glaciers are polluted and spit out corpses; political financing is corrupt; resources are consumed at three times a sustainable rate; global warming proceeds twice as quickly as the world average; convicted rapists walk the streets; prisons are disproportionately full of foreigners; tsunamis threaten its great lakes; and shit-soaked meadows are a disaster for biodiversity.

It is a country where cows dash off of cliffs and Kim Jong-un played with Legos; its teenagers lead the west in cannabis consumption and the world in avoiding pregnancy; it is a land-locked country with a navy, the source of Europe's four great rivers, and the blank spot in the middle of the EU. The clocks in its train stations are almost always wrong, its currency pays homage to a counterfeiter, its capital honors infant cannibalism, its center is in Italy, its air force goes to sleep at night, its dams could wrap a wall around the world, its scientists tinker with black holes, its power plants consume electricity, and rich troves of headless dinosaurs, stuck in the mud, predate its peaks.

Switzerland is *die Schweiz, la Suisse, Svizzera, Svizra, die Eidgenossenschaft,* and most correctly, in order not to favor any particular one of its four official languages, *Confoederatio*

Helvetica—personified in the female figure Helvetia who graces its coins. Helvetia comes from the Gaulish *elu-*, "prosperity," and *etu-*, meaning "grassland." Switzerland is a "prosperous and grassy land." First attested in 300 BC, this name still nails it after over two millennia.

Lightning Source UK Ltd.
Milton Keynes UK
UKHW012048101218
333786UK00001B/71/P